# THE EVOLUTION OF SINN FEIN

By
ROBERT MITCHELL HENRY

BOOKS FOR LIBRARIES PRESS
FREEPORT, NEW YORK

First Published 1920
Reprinted 1971

INTERNATIONAL STANDARD BOOK NUMBER:
0-8369-5625-7

LIBRARY OF CONGRESS CATALOG CARD NUMBER:
77-146858

PRINTED IN THE UNITED STATES OF AMERICA

# THE EVOLUTION
OF SINN FEIN

# CONTENTS

|  | Page |
|---|---|
| INTRODUCTORY | 1 |
| IRISH NATIONALISM IN THE NINETEENTH CENTURY SINN FEIN | 39 |
| THE EARLY YEARS OF SINN FEIN | 71 |
| SINN FEIN AND THE REPUBLICANS | 88 |
| THE VOLUNTEER MOVEMENT | 106 |
| ULSTER AND NATIONALIST IRELAND | 128 |
| SINN FEIN, 1914—1916 | 158 |
| AFTER THE RISING | 213 |
| CONCLUSION | 279 |

# THE EVOLUTION OF SINN FEIN

## INTRODUCTORY.

It is almost a commonplace of the political moralists that every failure on the part of England to satisfy the moderate and constitutional demands of the Irish people for reform has been followed invariably by a deplorable outbreak of "extremist" activities in Ireland. Unfortunately for the moral, that constitutional demands should therefore be promptly and fully conceded, the statement is almost exactly the reverse of the truth, if Irish history as a whole be taken as the field for induction. The Irish Nation cannot be said to have at any period abandoned its claim to independence. Of the meaning of that claim there was no question from the Conquest to the fall of Limerick. The whole of that period is occupied by a long struggle between the English and the Irish peoples for the effective possession of the island. On neither side was there any misapprehension of the meaning and object of the contest. The English Government, whether it employed naked force, intrigue or legal fiction, aimed (and was understood to aim) at the moral, material and political subjugation of the Irish: the Irish, whether they fought in the field or intrigued in the cabinets of Europe, whether allied with France or with Spain or English royalists, had but one object, the assertion of their national independence. It was a struggle not merely between two nations but between two civilizations. Men of English blood who were absorbed by the Irish nation and who accepted the Irish civilization fought as stoutly for the independence of their adopted (and adopting) country as did the descendants of the Milesians. England could never count on the fidelity to her ideals and policy in Ireland of the second generation of her own settlers. History cannot produce another instance of a struggle so prolonged and so pertinacious. Whole counties, stripped by fire and sword of their aboriginal owners, were repeopled within two or three generations and renewed the struggle. But superior numbers and organization, a more fortunate star and (it seemed) the designs of Providence, prevailed in the end; and with the fall of Limerick England might have regarded her task as at last accomplished. The Irish Nation was prostrate, and chains were forged for it which, heavier and more galling than any forged for any nation before, seemed to offer a perpetual guarantee of slavery, misery and degradation. Ireland was henceforth to be administered as a kind of convict settlement. The law, in the words of a famous judgment, did not presume the existence of such a person as a Catholic Irishman; that is to say, two-thirds of the inhabitants of the country had no legal existence. Legal existence was the privilege of Protestant Englishmen living in Ireland and of such Protestant Irishmen as claimed it. But legal existence in Ireland during the eighteenth century was no prize to be grasped at. The mere fact of residence in Ireland entailed practical disabilities for which no mere local ascendancy was an adequate compensation. The manufactures and trade of Ireland were systematically and ruthlessly suppressed. Englishmen who settled there found that while they were at liberty to oppress "the mere Irish" they were subject themselves to a similar oppression by the English who remained at home. No one might enter that prison house and remain wholly a man. The "garrison" grumbled, protested and threatened, but in vain. Constitutionalists appealed to the policy of the Conquest in support of the independence of the country. It was argued that the Parliament of Ireland, established by the conquerors as a symbol of annexation, was and ought to be independent of the Parliament of England. The claim was held to be baseless and treasonable; so far from being abandoned or weakened, it was enforced and asserted by the arms of the Volunteers, and in less than a century after the fall of Limerick the Renunciation Act of 1783 enacted that the people of Ireland should be " bound only by laws enacted by his Majesty and the parliament of that kingdom in all cases whatever."

But while this was independence, it was independence in the sense of Molyneux, Swift and Grattan, not in the sense in which it had been understood by Hugh O'Neill. The American colonies went farther and fared better, and the descendants of the race of Hugh O'Neill had to be reckoned with still. Their position under the settlement of 1783 was what it had been since the Treaty of Limerick was broken by the Penal Laws, and all that they gained at first was an indirect share in the prosperity which began for the country with the assertion of its legislative independence. The population increased; trade, commerce and manufactures flourished and multiplied; the flag of Ireland began once more to creep forth upon the seas; but the ancient race was still proscribed in the land of its birth. But while it was in human nature to invent, it was not in human nature to continue to administer, a code so diabolical as that of the Penal Laws. The Volunteers who claimed legislative independence of England asserted the rights of conscience for their fellow-countrymen. Under the free Parliament a gradual alleviation took place in the lot of Catholics in Ireland; in 1793 they were admitted to the franchise and there is a presumption that had the Irish Parliament really been independent the Penal Laws would have in time been abolished entirely. But the vigilance of English policy and English Ministers never ceased; their meddling in the affairs of Ireland was perpetual and mischievous: the rights of the Irish Parliament were constantly in danger from the interference of English Ministers who advised their common Monarch and moulded his Irish policy through the Viceroy and the Executive. It was but a step from the admission of Catholics to the franchise to their admission to the House of Commons, but that step was never taken by the Irish Parliament. The measures of Parliamentary reform pressed upon them by the popular party both inside and outside Parliament were constantly rejected, partly through the mere conservatism of privilege partly through the influence of the English Cabinet. The United Irishmen, whose aim was to establish a free and equal representation of all Irishmen irrespective of creed, despaired of obtaining their object by open agitation and, subjected to repressive enactments, transformed themselves into a secret association for the overthrow of the existing government and for complete separation from England as the only method of securing and maintaining the rights of Ireland. They were the first Irish Republican Party. They appealed for assistance to the French Directory, but so jealous were they of their independence that they seem to have jeopardized the prospect of help by their insistence that the force sent must not be large enough to threaten the subjugation of the country. The Government, becoming aware of the conspiracy, took steps at once to foster it and to crush it. Their agents went through the country, forming United Irish lodges and then denouncing the members to the authorities. Under pretence of helping the Irish Government in its difficulties, English regiments were poured into the country and, when a sufficient force was assembled, open rebellion was provoked and crushed with a systematic barbarity which is even now hardly credible.

To understand the Rebellion and the policy of the Union which followed it, one must go farther back than the last quarter of the eighteenth century. The fall of Limerick ended (or seemed to end) the struggle for the military domination of Ireland. Once it was in the effective possession of England the period of its commercial subjugation began. Every kind of manufacture which competed with that of England was suppressed: every branch of commerce which threatened rivalry with that of England was forbidden. To ensure at once that military resistance might not be renewed and that commercial subjugation might be endured the policy was adopted first (to quote Archbishop Boulter) of "filling the great places with natives of England" and secondly of perpetuating the animosity between Protestants and Catholics. It was hoped in this way to form "two nations" out of one and render the task of government and exploitation easier in consequence. The remarkable power of absorbing foreign settlers shown by the Irish Nation since before the Conquest was thus to be nullified and religion pressed into service against humanity. So clearly was this policy conceived that Archbishop Boulter could write " The worst of this is that it tends to unite Protestant with Papist and, whenever that happens, good-bye to the English interests in Ireland forever." But the agents of the policy overreached themselves. Irish Protestants turned against a policy which counted the merit of being a Protestant as less than the demerit of being Irish. Dean Swift won the favour alike of Irish Protestant and Irish Catholic by his mordant pamphlets against the English policy in Ireland and may justly be reckoned as on the whole the most powerful champion of Irish independence in the sense of the eighteenth century. The Irish agents of the policy of Protestant Ascendancy overreached themselves too. Official Irish Protestantism bore almost as hardly upon Presbyterians as upon Papists, and the United Irishmen at the end of the century found no support in Ireland warmer than that accorded them by the best of the Ulster Presbyterians. There is little doubt that the reversal of the commercial ascendancy by the legislation of 1782 was regarded by the English Ministry as a merely temporary setback, to be repaired at the earliest convenient opportunity. In any case the valuable asset of Protestant Ascendancy, with its possibilities of perpetual friction and disunion among Irishmen, was still in their hands. When the rise of the United Irishmen threatened even this, the necessity of recovering the lost ground and the opportunity of doing so were immediately recognised. The obstinacy with which the Irish Parliament opposed Parliamentary reform (an obstinacy directly fostered by

the policy of the English Ministry) drove the
United Irish movement into hostility at once to
the English connection and to the existing constitution of Ireland. They could thus be represented as at once a menace to England and a
menace to Ireland, and it was held to be the duty
of both Governments to combine to crush them.
They were crushed by English troops, but the Irish
Parliament was crushed with them. Pitt decided
that direct control by the English Ministry must
take the place of indirect control through an Irish
Executive, and the Legislative Union was enacted.
There seemed to be no other permanent or ultimate
alternative to the complete independence and
separation of England and Ireland.

Much impressive rhetoric has been expended
upon the measures taken to secure that the members of the Irish Parliament should produce a
majority in favour of the Act of Union. They
were bribed and intimidated; they were offered
posts and pensions: some of them were bought with
hard cash. But even a Castlereagh must have
been aware that if he should suborn a servant to
betray his master the gravamen of the charge
against him would not be that he had corrupted
the morals of the servant by offering him a bribe.
Ordinary morality may not apply to politics, but
if it does, Pitt and Castlereagh were guilty of a
far greater crime than that of bribing a few scores
of venal Irishmen; and the members of the Irish
Parliament who took their money were guilty not
of corruption but of treason. For the Act of

INTRODUCTORY 9

Union was intended to accomplish the destruction of the national existence. The members of Parliament who voted against it, knew this: the Irish people who petitioned against it, knew this: Pitt and Castlereagh knew it: the men they paid to vote for it, knew it too.

The politics of Ireland during the nineteenth century would have been tangled enough at the best, but the Act of Union introduced a confusion which has often seemed to make the situation inexplicable to a normal mind. But, to leave details aside, the main lines of the problem are clear enough. The Act of Union was designed to end the separate national existence of Ireland by incorporating its legislative and administrative machinery with that of England. To secure control to the "Predominant Partner" (as the incorporating body has since been called) the representation of Ireland in the Imperial Parliament was fixed at a total which at the time of the Act was less than half that to which it was entitled on the basis of the population. While the intention of the authors of the measure (as their published correspondence makes perfectly clear) was to subordinate Irish national interests to those of England, the measure was presented to Parliament as one designed to further the mutual interests of the two kingdoms. But to Protestant waverers it was commended in private as a necessary means of securing the Protestant interest, while to the Catholics hopes were held out that the removal of the Catholic disabilities maintained by the

Protestant ascendancy in Ireland might be hoped
for from the more liberal Parliament in England.
There is no doubt that many Catholics, especially
among the nobility and higher clergy, were induced at least to discourage resistance to the
measure, partly for this reason, partly out of fear
of the republican sympathies and aims of the
reforming United Irishmen. The extreme
Protestants, such as the Orangemen who helped
to suppress the rebellion, viewed the measure with
a certain suspicion, if not with definite hostility.
They looked forward, now that the rebellion was
crushed, to a prolonged tenure of unchallenged
ascendancy. But the bulk of the more liberal
Protestants were against it, and the wiser
Catholics. They foretold the ruin of trade, the
burden of increased taxation, the loss of all real
independence and freedom that were bound to, and
did, result. But they were neither consulted nor
listened to and the measure was passed after free
speech had been bought over in Parliament and
suppressed by military force outside.

The measure once passed brought about an unnatural shifting of parties in Ireland. Many of
those who had opposed the measure before it
became law, now decided to make the best of what
could no longer be prevented. The orators of the
Patriot Party passed over to the English Parliament and were practically lost to Ireland. The
aristocracy who had upheld the Irish Parliament
gravitated towards the new seat of Government
and abandoned a capital deserted by the Parlia-

## INTRODUCTORY 11

ment of their pride. They sent their children to be educated in England, and in the second generation they began to call themselves not Irishmen but Englishmen. The representatives of both these parties became in time convinced upholders of the Union and their influence in Ireland was thrown in favour of the maintenance of the *status quo*. To this " Unionist" party must be added the Orange party who stood for Protestant ascendancy. Much as they disliked the Union to begin with they came to see in the end that, unaided, they could not stand for long against the claim of their Catholic fellow-countrymen for political equality. The one thing that reconciled them to the Union was its possibilities in securing the Protestant interest. To this attitude they have remained faithful ever since, and in the course of the century they were joined by the majority of the Protestants of Ireland. Ulster, at one time the chief strength of the United Irishmen, became the headquarters of extreme and even fanatical support of the Union. Here " the Protestant interest," carefully fostered as an instrument of English influence in Ireland, founded its citadel, the rallying point of opposition to " Irish" claims. After Connaught, the most definitely "Celtic" portion of Ireland (in spite of the Ulster Plantations), its extreme Protestant sympathies, carefully fostered by the Protestant clergy into a bigotry that has become grotesque, converted the dominions of the O'Neills and the O'Donnells into a desperate and apparently irreconcilable antagonist of Irish national interests. Besides, Ulster suffered less than the rest of Ireland from the economic effects of the Union. Though the population of Ulster has been almost halved as the result of it, the "Ulster custom" saved the tenants from some of the worst abuses of the land system of the other provinces, and the prosperity of the linen trade, never endangered by collision with English interests, did not suffer by the measure; while the greater wealth of the manufacturing districts made the burden of unfair taxation (which repressed commercial and industrial enterprise in the rest of Ireland) less felt than it might have been. A mistaken view of their own interests, and an equally mistaken view of the real aims of the rest of their countrymen (a mistake sometimes encouraged by the tactics of their opponents) converted Protestant Ulster into an attitude which ignorance has represented as a consciousness of a racial difference between itself and the rest of Ireland. But even in Ulster there still remain many Protestant Irishmen to whom the recollection of the days of the United Irishmen is like the recollection of the Golden Age. Still faithful to the doctrines of equality, fraternity and freedom they are the last links of the chain which once bound Ulster to the cause of Ireland.

On the other hand Catholic Ireland as a whole, and especially its leaders, ecclesiastical and other, viewed the enactment of the legislative Union with a kind of apathetic despair. Nothing apparently was to be hoped from the Irish Parliament in the direction of real religious equality or reform of the franchise: nothing more could be expected from armed resistance after the signal failure of the rebellion. The country was occupied by an English army and, whatever they thought, they must think in silence. Hopes were held out that the Union might bring Catholic Emancipation, that the Catholic clergy might receive a State subsidy similar to that given to the Presbyterian ministers. They were to find that Catholic Emancipation was no more to the taste of England than to that of the Irish Parliament and that a State subsidy to the Catholic Church would only be granted at the price which Castlereagh desired the Presbyterian ministers to pay for the *Regium Donum*. But for the moment they did nothing and there was nothing that could be done. Entitled to vote but not to sit in Parliament, but half-emancipated from the bondage, material and moral, of the Penal Laws, they had no effective weapon at their disposal within the constitution, and the only other weapon that they had had broken in their hands. They were forced into a position of silent and half-hearted protest, and have ever since been at the disadvantage of having to appear as the disturbers of the existing order. The hopes held out by the promoters of the Union were not realized without prolonged and violent agitation, and the cause of Ireland appeared doubly alien, clothed in the garb of a Church alien to the legislators to whom appeal was made. That the national cause was first identified with the claims of Irish Catholics to religious equality is the *damnosa hereditas* of Irish Nationalism in the nineteenth century. The music of " the Pope's Brass Band" drowns the voice of orator and poet. The demand that the nation as a whole should no longer be compelled to support the establishment of the Church of a minority was represented as a move on the part of the Roman Curia to cripple Protestantism in the United Kingdom. The demand for the reform of the worst land system in Europe was looked upon as a resistance to the constitution inspired by the agents of the Vatican. The Irish people asks for nothing, but the Pope or the Irish Catholic hierarchy, working in darkness, is supposed to have put it into their heads, though the Irish people have taught both Pope and Bishops many lessons upon the distinction between religious authority and political dictation.

Thus there gradually developed during the nineteenth century the Unionist and the Nationalist parties, the former upholding the legislative Union though not averse (upon pressure) to the concession of administrative reforms: the latter under many forms claiming in greater or lesser measure the abolition of the *fons et origo malorum*, the withdrawal from the people of Ireland of the right to an independent legislature. The historic claim to complete independence has on many occasions been modified in theory or abated in practice by the National leaders: but a survey of the history of Ireland since the Union shows that, with whatever apparent abatements or disguises the claim may have been pressed, there has always been deep down the feeling that behind the Union lay the Conquest, the hope that to repeal the one meant a step upon the road to annul the other.

# IRISH NATIONALISM IN THE NINE-
TEENTH CENTURY.

The political history of Post-Union Ireland opens with an armed rebellion. Robert Emmet for an abortive attempt to seize Dublin Castle was condemned and executed in 1803. His rising was the last effort of the United Irishmen. Since the Union, and for more than a century after his death, the country was governed under a species of martial law, and Coercion Acts were matters of almost annual enactment. The Government could not count on the steady loyalty of any class of the community. The Orange societies required to be placated, the Presbyterians to be muzzled, the Catholics to be suppressed. Castlereagh's administration was a frank recognition of the fact that Irishmen as a body were hostile to the Union, and that any means might be employed to keep them quiet. For more than twenty years the Catholics waited in vain for the fulfilment of the hopes of emancipation held out at the time of the Union. Meanwhile "the bonds of Empire" continued to be drawn tighter and tighter. In 1817 the Irish Exchequer, the belated relic of Ireland's independent existence, was amalgamated with that of England, and the long history of the financial oppression of the country began. At

last in 1823 Catholic Ireland began the public
agitation of its claims for civil equality with Irish
Protestants. The agitation, justifiable and necessary in itself, natural and dignified had it taken
place in an independent Ireland and had it been
of the nature of an appeal to the justice of their
fellow-countrymen, assumed the inevitable form of
an appeal to a foreign legislature for a justice
denied them at home. The Catholic Association
founded in 1760 was revived by Daniel O'Connell
and in six years' time, so strong was the feeling
aroused, the English Government yielded, for fear
(as the Duke of Wellington confessed) of a civil
war. O'Connell had talked as if he were ready
for anything and the Duke of Wellington seems
to have thought that he meant what he said. It
was the first victory for " moral force " and
O'Connell became enamoured of the new weapon.
Next year the Tithe War broke out and ended in
1838 in an incomplete victory, the Tithes, instead
of being abolished, being paid henceforth in money
as an addition to the rent. But before the Tithe
War ended, O'Connell (now member for Clare in
the Imperial Parliament) had founded the Constitutional Party by giving his support to Lord
Melbourne's Government. For O'Connell's policy
there was this to be said: that, the Union being
an accomplished fact, the only way to secure legislative benefits for Ireland was through the only
means recognized by the constitution: that, both
English parties being equally indifferent to the
special interests of Ireland, it was sound practical

policy to secure by an alliance with one or other,
as occasion might dictate, some special claim upon
its consideration and (incidentally) some hope of
appointments to Government positions of Irishmen
in sympathy with the majority in Ireland: that the
only alternative was open defiance of the Constitution and the sacrifice of what otherwise might be
gained by its recognition. Against his policy it
could be urged that to employ constitutional forms
was to recognize a constitution repugnant to his
declared convictions; that appeals to the Parliament of the United Kingdom tended in practice to
intensify Irish divisions and to break up the
nation into two groups of litigants pleading before
a bar which viewed them with an indifferent
disdain; that in any case success in the appeal
would be the result of accident and circumstance
or be dictated by the interests of English policy.
Between these two views of Irish national policy
Ireland has been divided and has wavered ever
since.

But O'Connell, having been successful once,
seems to have conceived it possible to be successful
always, and he decided to attempt the Repeal of
the Union. It is hard to suppose that he thought
this possible by any means which he was prepared
to use. In 1840 he founded the Repeal Association. and in two years' time he had practically the
whole of Catholic Ireland, and a small but
enthusiastic body of Protestants, behind him.
Monster meetings were held all over the country.
Repeal Clubs were founded, recruits pressed in,

"moral force," in the form of threats that "he would either be in his grave or a freeman" within a reasonable time, was employed by the leader. But when the Government proclaimed the meeting, announced to be held on Sunday, October the 8th, 1843, at Clontarf, chosen as the scene of Brian Boroimhe's crowning victory over the Danes, O'Connell yielded at discretion. No reform, as he proclaimed afterwards, was worth the shedding of a single drop of human blood; and Brian's battlefield saw the troops wait all day long for the foe that never came. Unable to persuade, O'Connell was unprepared to fight, the enemies of Repeal. But the Repeal Association continued: the Repeal members of Parliament either were (like O'Connell) arrested and imprisoned or withdrew from Westminster to deliberate in Ireland upon Committees of the Repeal Association on matters of national moment. As time went on, O'Connell (and still more his worthless son, John) gave the Association an ever-increasing bias towards sectarianism and away from Nationalism. He fought the "Young Ireland" Party, as Davis, Gavan Duffy, John Mitchel and their associates were called, who carried on the purely national and liberal traditions of the United Irishmen, and finally forced them to secede. Their paper *The Nation*, founded in 1842, was until its suppression the mouthpiece of the liberal and really National Party. It voiced in impassioned prose and verse the aspirations of the historic Irish nation. Its guiding spirit, Thomas Davis, was a member of

a Protestant family in Mallow, and its contributors
comprised men of all creeds, Irish and Anglo-Irish,
who looked forward to the revival of Irish culture,
of the Irish language and of an Irish polity in
which room would be found for all sons and
daughters of Ireland, free to develop as one of the
family of European nations, released from all outside interference in national concerns.  But Irish
divisions, fostered by the Union, fomented by
statecraft and furthered by many Irishmen, grew
steadily more pronounced.  Thomas Davis and his
friends, at the risk of misunderstanding and mis-
representation, did their utmost to promote union
on the basis of a common pride in Ireland's past
and a common hope for Ireland's future.  The
Committees of the Repeal Association worked hard
at reports upon Irish needs and Irish conditions.
They promoted the composition and publication of
Repeal Essays pointing to the results of the Union
in diminishing manufactures and in an impoverished national life.  They had a temporary
success, and their writings were destined to supply
inspiration to their successors, but they were
battling with a running tide.  The moderate
people, tired of the struggle, were finding in
Federalism a resting place between conviction and
expediency or had made up their minds to accept
the Union.  The gradual process of Anglicization
went on apace.  The establishment in 1831 of the
Board of National Education under the joint
management of Catholic, Protestant and Presbyterian dignitaries was, in spite of much opposition,

making sure headway. It was destined to destroy
for all practical purposes the Gaelic language
which till then had been in common use in all
parts of Ireland. It proscribed Irish history and
Irish patriotic poetry in its schools. It was seized
upon by ecclesiastics of all persuasions and made,
in the name of religion, a potent instrument of
a policy of internal division and mistrust. It placed
education, with all its possibilities of national
culture and national union, in the hands of a Board
definitely anti-national in its outlook, working
through instruments to whom sectarian prejudices
meant more than national welfare. Had Davis
lived he might have done much with his great
gifts, his tolerant spirit and his heroic temper: his
death in 1845 was one of the greatest losses which
Ireland suffered during the nineteenth century.
O'Connell, whose later activities had been almost
wholly mischievous, died two years later just as
the full horror of the Famine burst upon the
country. The Government which had assumed
responsibility for the interests of Ireland, met this
awful visitation with an ineptitude so callous as
almost to justify John Mitchel's fiercest denunciations. While the crops were being exported from
the country over 700,000 persons died of starvation
and as many again by famine fever. When the
fever and famine had done their work, the clearances began. The population fled from the
country where there was nothing left for them
or, if they did not fly, they were shipped off by
the landlords to leave room for the development of

grazing farms. From 1846 to 1851, one million
and a quarter of the population "emigrated," and
in the next nine years they were followed, thanks
to the same causes, by another million and a half.
During the same period 373,000 families were
evicted from their holdings to provide room for a
handful of graziers.

The Famine and its consequences seemed a final
proof of the failure of the English Government to
preserve the elementary interests of Ireland, and
a section of the Young Irelanders could see no
other remedy than an appeal to force, if they were
to regain independence and keep Ireland from
destruction. John Mitchel seceded from *The
Nation* and founded *The United Irishman*, in
which week after week with extraordinary eloquence and courage he advocated the policy of
resistance. He advised the peasantry to procure
arms, to manufacture pikes, if nothing better could
be had, to resist the official searches for arms (for
a stringent Coercion Act had been one of the
weapons with which the Government combatted
the Famine) and to refuse to allow food to leave
the country. He appealed in a series of letters to
the Protestant farmers of Ulster to help Ireland
as they had helped before in the days of the United
Irishmen. Had all the leaders of the Young
Ireland Party possessed the spirit of Mitchel, and
had any of them known how to organize a rebellion, they would not have lacked a very formidable
following. But Mitchel was arrested, sentenced
and transported before anything was done and the

## IRISH NATIONALISM IN THE 19TH CENTURY 23

actual outbreak under Smith O'Brien and Meagher was doomed to failure from the outset.

Mitchel had advanced far beyond "moral force" and the Repeal of the Union. He had definitely renounced the idea of arguing the Union out of existence: he regarded no policy as either practicable or manly which did not begin and end in the assertion that Ireland was a free country and was prepared to adopt any and every means to put her freedom into practice. Like all the Young Irelanders, he had begun his political life as a Repealer and a follower of O'Connell; he had appealed to the Irish gentry to act again as they had acted in 1782. But Irish history since the Union and especially the experiences of the Famine years (there had been several partial famines before 1846) was making some serious thinkers very sceptical of a political solution which left one of the main factors of politics out of account. The man who saw the defects of the Repeal solution and exposed them most trenchantly and convincingly was James Fintan Lalor. In a series of letters and articles written for *The Nation* and for the *Irish Felon* he expounded a theory of nationality which went to the very roots of political facts. His policy was not Repeal; "I will never," he said, "contribute one shilling or give my name, heart, or hand, for such an object as the simple repeal by the British Parliament of the Act of Union." The facts of everyday life in Ireland showed that a new social system was required. the old having had its day. "There was no outrise or revolt against it. It was not broken up by violence. It was borne for ages with beggarly patience, until it perished by the irritation of God in the order of nature." So long as a system remained in which the land of Ireland was not in possession of the people of Ireland, no repeal or other measure purely political would avail. If the landlords were to remain (and Lalor had no desire to expel them if they were willing to submit to the paramount right of the nation) they must accept their titles to whatever rights should be theirs from the Irish nation and the Irish nation only. " The principle I state, and mean to stand upon, is this" (he wrote) " that the entire ownership of Ireland, moral and material, up to the sun and down to the centre, is vested of right in the people of Ireland; that they, and none but they, are the landowners and lawmakers of this island; that all laws are null and void not made by them, and all titles to land invalid not conferred and confirmed by them; and that this full right of ownership may and ought to be asserted and enforced by any and all means which God has put in the power of man." The coming of the lean years culminating in the Famine had taught Lalor the overwhelming importance of the question: "A revolution is beginning to begin which will leave Ireland *without a people* unless it be met and conquered by a revolution which will leave it without landlords." Failure to observe (or to see the importance of) the land question had led to the defeat of Mitchel and Smith O'Brien. " They wanted

an alliance with the landowners. They chose to
consider them as Irishmen, and imagined they
could induce them to hoist the green flag. They
wished to preserve an Aristocracy. They desired,
not a democratic, but merely a national revolution. Who imputes blame to them for this?
Whoever does so will not have me to join him. I
have no feeling but one of respect for the motives
that caused reluctance and delay. That delay,
however, I consider as a matter of deep regret.
Had the Confederation, in the May or June of '47,
thrown heart and mind and means and might into
the movement I pointed out, they would have made
it successful, and settled at once and for ever all
quarrels and questions between us and England."
But though Lalor insisted on the importance of
the question of the ownership of the soil and confessed complete indifference to Repeal, an indifference which he claimed was largely shared by
the people of Ireland (for Repeal, as he said, the
Irish wolf dog " will never bite, but only bark")
he was a land reformer, not out of a lack of interest
in political questions, but out of an intense belief
in the realities of politics. He never joined the
Repealers, partly because O'Connell and his following disgusted him; as he says in a letter to
Gavan Duffy: " Before I embarked in the boat I
looked at the crew and the commander; the same
boat which you and others mistook in '43 for a
war frigate because she hoisted gaudy colours and
that her captain swore terribly. I knew her at
once for a leaky collier-smack, with a craven crew

to man her, and a sworn dastard and a foresworn traitor at the helm—a fact which you and Young Ireland would seem never to have discovered until he ordered the boat to be stranded and yourselves to be set ashore." This language may be unnecessarily vigorous and hurtful but the judgment is not essentially unjust. But it was not merely disgust which kept Lalor out of the Repeal ranks. He disbelieved utterly in the Repeal of the Union as a solution for the Irish question. It was in the first place impracticable. " You will *NEVER*, in form of law, repeal the Act of Union. *Never*, while the sun sits in heaven, and the laws of nature are in action. *Never*, before night goes down on the last day." What was, however, practicable was to claim the land, refuse to pay rent for it, and institute a protracted, obstinate and violent resistance to the attempt on the part of English troops to take it back again. Once the land was again in the possession of the people of Ireland their ultimate policy would be clear. " Not the repeal of the Union, then, but the Conquest—not to disturb or dismantle the Empire, but to abolish it utterly for ever—not to fall back on '82 but act up to '48—not to resume or restore an old constitution, but found a new nation and raise up a free people, and strong as well as free, and secure as well as strong, based on a peasantry rooted like rocks in the soil of the land—this is my object."
" Not the constitution that Wolfe Tone died to abolish, but the constitution that Wolfe Tone died to obtain—independence; full and absolute inde-

pendence for this island, and for every man within this island." Lalor knew well enough that this meant fighting in the long run, but he thought that it was worth fighting for while Repeal of the Union was not: but who was to lead the fight? Little was to be looked for from the Repeal leaders, content with " a small Dublin reputation," with neither the desire nor the talents to lead a nation. His last article in the *Irish Felon*, written while Smith O'Brien and Meagher were in prison, is an impassioned appeal for someone to lead a nation that was only waiting for a man. " Remember this—that somewhere and somehow and by somebody, a beginning must be made. Who strikes the first blow for Ireland? Who draws first blood for Ireland? Who wins a wreath that will be green for ever?"

The *perenni fronde corona* which Lalor promised has not yet been won and may never be won by the means which Lalor thought of, but the influence of his writings upon later Irish political thought has been profound. The Repeal Movement brought out three men of real genius—Davis, Mitchel and Lalor. Davis was always more than a simple Repealer; his mind took in too great a range, his knowledge was too wide, his commonsense too great, to see in Repeal of the Union the ultimate end of Irish political endeavour. Mitchel abandoned Repeal for Revolution in hot blood and out of a haughty heart. Lalor had the cool head and the keen eye and the sense of reality which Mitchel lacked: but though he wrote less and did less and suffered less, what he lost in immediate reputation he gained in his influence over a later age and in a wider field.

The situation of Ireland in the years immediately following the Famine was tragic. On the one side was starvation, impotence, despair. The starvation might have been, and in any normally governed country would have been, averted: but Ireland was in the unnatural position of being governed by outsiders who had absolutely no interest in the country beyond that of ensuring that it should not govern itself: seeing the remedy for its misery, but unable to employ it, in the face of an army which not all the fiery eloquence of Mitchel and Meagher could persuade the starving people was capable of being defeated by a mob of pikemen, Ireland sank back into an apathetic and moody despair from which it took many years to recover, during which the life of the nation almost drained away. On the other side was the Government, indifferent to the misery of its victim, determined that nothing, not even the extinction of the race, should alter the fixed resolve of England to be absolute and sole master in Ireland. The failure of the Rebellion of '48 was not to the rulers of England a matter altogether of congratulation. A highly-placed personage, able to gauge with accuracy the sentiment of the English ruling classes, wrote: "There are ample means of crushing the rebellion in Ireland and I think it is now very likely to go off without any contest, which people (and I think with right) rather regret. The

# IRISH NATIONALISM IN THE 19TH CENTURY

Irish should receive a good lesson or they will begin again." The awful mortality from famine and pestilence was regarded with a kind of chastened and reverential gratitude, as an unexpected interference of Providence for the extirpation of the hated race. In the then temper of England no revolution had the least chance of sympathy or success. It would have been crushed, whatever the cost.

But though prostrate, despairing and depleted Ireland still claimed her rights, though for a few years it seemed as if they had been tacitly waived. The Repeal agitation died, and its place was taken by the Irish Tenant League which aimed not at interference with constitutional arrangements but at the solution of the land question, not in the radical method advocated by Lalor but by legislation securing certain rights to the tenant, the claim of the landlord to be owner of the land being left untouched. Lalor had foretold that on the land question Ulster instead of being " on the flank" of the rest of Ireland would march with it side by side: and Gavan Duffy in his League of the North and South went some length in the way of securing the co-operation of the Northern Tenant Righters. At the same time the Irish representatives in Parliament formed the beginning of an Independent Parliamentary Party, holding aloof from any binding alliance with either English Party but combining at need with the party most favourable at the moment to Irish claims. But the new policy proved a failure within three years, partly by the treachery of members of the party, but chiefly through the inherent hopelessness of the position of any Irish party then in Parliament. Besides, the Tenant League had to contend with the masterful personality of Cardinal Cullen, an ecclesiastic of the Ultramontane School, who spent his life in the endeavour, temporarily successful, to throw the whole weight of his Church against the just claims of the nation.

During the abortive attempt at a constitutional policy, the survivors of the party of Mitchel and Lalor were not idle. It cannot be said that Ireland had at this time come to recognize the futility of parliamentary agitation, for it cannot be said to have given it a sufficient trial: but the results of it had so far been disappointing, and the tradition of independence was still fresh, and its spirit strong. The new form which was assumed by the Separatist movement after the failure of '48 was that known as the Fenian Society, or the Irish Republican Brotherhood. Its chief organizers, James Stephens, John O'Mahony, John O'Leary and Thos. Clarke Luby had all been " out" in '48. Stephens and O'Mahony had lived in Paris till 1850; Stephens then returned to Ireland, gaining his living as a teacher of French, while O'Mahony went to New York. Both in Ireland and New York the teaching of the two friends found ready listeners, and an amazing success. The Irish in America were only too ready to return to Ireland to overthrow the Government in whose authority they saw the source of their country's misfortunes

# IRISH NATIONALISM IN THE 19TH CENTURY 31

and their own exile. On the conclusion of the American War thousands of Irishmen who had fought under Grant or Jackson were ready to place their services at the disposal of an Irish leader. But they found no one of sufficient ability and prestige to lead them. Smith O'Brien and the other survivors of the Young Ireland Party had become constitutionalists. John Mitchel, though he went to Paris to act as treasurer for the Society, refused to take any more active part. O'Mahony and the Americans wanted to equip and despatch an expedition: James Stephens, who had undertaken to organize the movement in Ireland, insisted that American assistance should be confined to money. The money came in slowly and though Stephens could enrol a revolutionary army he could not equip it. The Americans too wanted the rising to take place before Stephens thought the time was ripe, and the consequent quarrel between the Irish and American leaders was fatal to the chance of success. In any case little real progress was made until the year 1865, but the work of preparation went steadily on. The organization in Ireland, which at first was without a name, the oath of membership being merely an oath of allegiance to the Irish Republic, was formally inaugurated on St. Patrick's Day, 1858. In 1859 the Government, becoming alarmed, broke up the Phœnix Society of Skibbereen, an independent organization, and the members later on joined the Fenians. All the forces of the Church and the influence of such recognized leaders as were left

were arrayed against the new organization.
Fenians were refused the rites of the Church for
being members of a secret oath-bound society, and
at least one member has left upon record that
having to choose between Faith and Country he
chose Country. The Fenians boldly defied
Cardinal Cullen and his clerical agents. The
*Irish People*, founded in 1862 under John O'Leary
as editor, took up the Cardinal's challenge and
faced consistently and courageously the question of
"the priest in politics." It did incalculable
service to the Fenians by its courage and frankness. In the same year Belfast and Ulster were
brought within the Fenian Circle. By 1865 there
were, it was claimed, 13,000 sworn Fenians in the
army, rather more in the militia, and a good
many of the police had joined as well. Stephens
judged it time to prepare for action, but his
despatches to the country ordering preparations to
begin fell into the hands of the police. The office
of the *Irish People* was seized, Habeas Corpus was
suspended and the jails were filled. Stephens himself was arrested some weeks afterwards. After
his escape from Richmond Prison he lay hid for
three months in Ireland and then escaped to France
and America. Whether better fortune would
have crowned his work if he had gone on in spite
of the arrests is a nice question. Some at any rate
of his followers judged that he had missed his
chance. The subsequent attempt in '67 under
American leaders fared no better; and General
Massey, arrested at Limerick Junction, judged it

## IRISH NATIONALISM IN THE 19TH CENTURY  33

better to avoid bloodshed by giving full information to the Government.

The Fenian Movement, as it was called, was both in Ireland and America avowedly republican and separatist from the very first. Stephens wished to establish one form of government only—an Irish Republic, and he believed in only one method —that of armed revolution. He refused steadily to have anything to do with tenant rights or parliamentary parties or tactics.

The avowed object of the Republican Brotherhood had failed, but it brought about two measures of Irish reform, long agitated and overdue, but neglected until the events of '65 and '67 brought home to a disdainful Parliament the realities of the abuses and of the feelings which their continuance had aroused. The Irish Church Act and Mr. Gladstone's first Land Bill were due to the Fenians. They were not formally concessions to Fenianism, as the Fenians were concerned first of all to establish a Republic and then to decide upon reforms for themselves; the Government merely supposed that by mending two intolerable abuses they could cut the ground from under the revolutionary movement. This policy could be only partially successful: but it succeeded so far that for a period of thirty years there was no Irish party that openly and consistently proclaimed its adhesion to the doctrine of complete separation.

The Home Rule policy put forward by Isaac Butt in 1870 fell far short even of O'Connell's Repeal. Its object was to set up, not an independent, but a strictly subordinate, Parliament in Dublin: the effect of this proposal (whatever its authors may have intended) would have been to consolidate the Union by removing opportunities of friction and of discontent. But even the appearance of a reversal of the policy of the Union was distasteful to Parliament; and the Irish members exhausted themselves in providing an annual exhibition of eloquence and passion for the delectation of a languid or tolerant audience. The pathetic and humiliating performance was ended by the appearance of Charles Stewart Parnell who infused into the forms of Parliamentary action the sacred fury of battle. He determined that Ireland, refused the right of managing her own destinies, should at least hamper the English in the government of their own house: he struck at the dignity of Parliament and wounded the susceptibilities of Englishmen by his assault upon the institution of which they are most justly proud. His policy of parliamentary obstruction went hand in hand with an advanced land agitation at home. The remnant of the Fenian Party rallied to his cause and suspended for the time, in his interests and in furtherance of his policy, their revolutionary activities. For Parnell appealed to them by his honest declaration of his intentions: he made it plain both to Ireland and to the Irish in America that his policy was no mere attempt at a readjustment of details in Anglo-Irish relations but the first step on the road to national independence. He was strong enough both to announce his ultimate intentions and to define with precision the limit which must be placed upon the immediate measures to be taken. During the years in which he was at the head of the National Movement practically all sections of Nationalists acknowledged his leadership and his policy. If he was not able to control all the extreme elements that grouped themselves under his banner it was no more than might have been expected. Neither he nor the Irish Republican Brotherhood was responsible for the murders perpetrated by the Invincibles, who had no connection or sympathy with the Fenian policy; but their excesses were used, and used with effect, to damage not only Parnell's position but the claims of Ireland. It was he himself who gave to his enemies in the end the only fatal weapon which they could use against him: but the prompt use of it by his own party was a portentous event in Irish politics. For the first time the Irish people not alone conformed to the exigencies of an alliance with an English party, but allowed that party to veto their choice of a leader. Parnell himself had once said " As the air of London would eat away the stone walls of the House of Commons, so would the atmosphere of the House eat away the honour and honesty of the Irish members." Certainly the tortuous ways of party politics had destroyed their loyalty, and though a small band proved faithful to him in spite of the Liberal veto, the majority came to a decision, practically dictated by the Irish hierarchy and acquiesced in (even if

reluctantly) by a majority of his countrymen, to
terminate his position as leader. But, though
this betrayal seemed to have destroyed the cause
for which he had fought, it may be questioned
whether it was really more than a symptom of the
inherent weakness of his position. The utmost he
could gain in the direction of Home Rule, the
utmost anyone could have gained under the
limitations which he himself imposed upon his
policy, fell markedly short of the minimum which
a majority of his followers thought attainable at
once and of what he himself announced to be the
ultimate object of his policy. He is remembered,
not as the leader who helped to force a Liberal
Government to produce two Home Rule Bills, but
as the leader who said " No man can set bounds
to the march of a nation."

The death of Parnell marks the end of an epoch.
A strong, romantic and mysterious personality, he
won and kept the affections of the Irish people in
a way which had been possible to few leaders before
him and which none has attained since. The
history of Irish politics for years after his death
was a story largely of small intrigue, base person-
alities, divided counsels and despairing expedients;
and the policy which eventually emerged, for
which Mr. John Redmond was responsible, was
widely removed from that of Parnell. The policy
to which Mr. Redmond's adhesion was given was
that of a Home Rule which might be described
as " Home Rule within the Union," a Home Rule
which in return for a local legislature and internal

control, resigned to the Imperial Parliament all
claim to the right to a foreign policy and to all
that would raise Ireland above the level of an
inferior dependency. It is true that Parnell
would have obtained little more than this, if he
had lived; but he would have obtained it in a
different way and would have accepted the concession with a gesture of independence. Post-
Parnellite Home Rule has been based largely upon
the ground that a better understanding between
the two countries is desirable in the interests of
both; that government in Ireland is less efficient,
more costly, less appreciated than it would be if it
were administered by the people of Ireland themselves, with a due regard to the interests and
general policy of the Empire; its justification is
found in the success of the self-governing colonies
who, thanks to being responsible for their own
affairs, are contented, prosperous and loyal part-
ners in an Imperial Commonwealth. All this is
true, but it is a truth that would have carried no
meaning to the mind of Parnell. To him the
British Empire was an abstraction in which Ireland had no spiritual concern; it formed part of
the order of the material world in which Ireland
found a place; it had, like the climatic conditions
of Europe, or the Gulf Stream, a real and pre-
ponderating influence on the destinies of Ireland.
But the Irish claim was to him the claim of a
nation to its inherent rights, not the claim of a portion of an empire to its share in the benefits which
the constitution of that empire bestowed upon its

more favoured parts. For some years after Parnell's death the leaders of the Irish Parliamentary Party felt obliged to maintain the continuity of tradition by using the language of the claim for independence and to speak of " severing the last link" which bound Ireland to England; but even in America and Ireland such expressions were heard less and less often from official Nationalists. The final attitude of the Irish Parliamentary Party is admirably summed up in the words of Mr. John Redmond : " Our demand for Home Rule does not mean that we want to break with the British Empire. We are entirely loyal to the Empire as such and we desire to strengthen the Imperial bonds through a liberal system of government. We do not demand such complete local autonomy as the British self-governing colonies possess, for we are willing to forego the right to make our own tariffs and are prepared to abide by any fiscal system enacted by the British Parliament . . . . Once we receive Home Rule we shall demonstrate our imperial loyalty beyond question."

Ten years before these words were used the Sinn Fein movement had begun, as a protest against the conception of national rights which made such language possible, as the latest form which the assertion of national independence has assumed.

# SINN FEIN.

Of the origin of this name as the title of a political party a pleasant tale is told. It is said that some people, convinced that (in the words of Davis) "the freeman's friend is Self-Reliance," and wishing to make it the basis of a national movement, being anxious for a suitable Irish name for such an idea, applied to a famous Irish scholar to furnish it. He told them a story of a country servant in Munster sent with a horse to the fair. The horse was sold and the servant after some days appeared in his master's kitchen, worn out but happy, and seated himself on the floor. To the enquiries of some neighbours who happened to be there, as to where he had been and what he had done, he would give no answer but "Sinn fein sinn fein." The prodigal servant's witty reply eludes the translator. To his hearers it conveyed that family matters were matters for the family: but it was no mere evasion of a temporary or personal difficulty. It was the expression of a universal truth. Society is divided into groups, large or small, which have their own problems and their own interests. Their problems they can best solve themselves, and of their interests they are themselves the best judges. The solutions and the judgments will not always commend themselves to outsiders; but though outsiders cannot be denied the right to hold and to express their opinions they have no rights of veto or of interference. This right of independence, however, is subject in practice to serious limitations, and the history of human society is largely the history of the reconciliation of the competing interests and claims of social groups, each claiming to be in the last resort rightfully independent. One of such groups is the nation, and it is generally recognized that nations as such have rights analogous to those exercised by other social groups. They may be forcibly deprived by another and stronger group of rights the exercise of which seems to the stronger to be inimical to its own interests; or rights may be surrendered in return for what may be judged to be a fair equivalent. But it is not held that rights can be extinguished by force or that, if a suitable opportunity should occur, they may not be regained either by force or by agreement. These things are generally acknowledged in the abstract; but in concrete instances there is seldom an equal unanimity: and a nation whose rights are in abeyance (especially if it be in the interest of a stronger neighbour-to prevent their exercise) is in a position which seldom admits of a simple or harmonious solution. Ideally it has a right to complete independence: practically it has to be content with as much independence as it can make good; and the methods which it may employ are various, always open to challenge and compassed by uncertainty.

A nation may maintain its moral and spiritual,

long after it has forfeited its material and political, independence. To such a nation the more valuable part of its independence has been preserved. But it is hardly possible in the long run for a nation which has become materially and politically dependent upon another to retain its moral and spiritual independence unimpaired. The loss of the latter is the final stage in national decline.

To the founders of Sinn Fein a national condition was presented to which no other remedy than their own seemed to offer the prospect of relief. All previous efforts to recover the political independence lost by the Act of Union had ended in disaster and disappointment. Force had been tried and proved unavailing: the experiences of '48 and '67 had left little doubt upon the minds of reasonable men that the attempt to regain Irish independence by force of arms was (however heroic) an impossible and foolish attempt. "We believe" (wrote the chief exponent of Sinn Fein) " with the editor of the *Irish World* that the four-and-a-quarter millions of unarmed people in Ireland would be no match in the field for the British Empire. If we did not believe so, as firmly as we believe the eighty Irishmen in the British House of Commons are no match for the six hundred Britishers opposed to them, our proper residence would be a padded cell." But if force of arms had proved useless, so had constitutional agitation. There was no argument of public justice, public expediency or public generosity which had not been urged without effect upon

Parliament. Irish members had been arguing against the Union for a hundred years: there was no point of view from which the case could be presented that had been overlooked. When Parliament seemed to listen and to be prepared to act it was found not to have heard the arguments for independence but arguments for a different kind of a Union. The belief that nothing was to be expected from Parliamentary action received later a striking confirmation: for when the Irish demand was whittled down to a bare minimum and all claim to independence expressly renounced, a pretext was found in the exigencies of English political relationships for refusing even that.

Not only had political independence gone beyond the chance of recovery by either force or argument but material independence had followed it. The trade, commerce and industries of Ireland which had flourished during its brief period of independence had dwindled since the Union and from causes for which the Union was directly responsible. The "equitable proportion" of Imperial taxation to which the taxes of Ireland had been restricted by the terms of the Act of Union had proved to be inequitable, so that Ireland was overtaxed to the extent of two-and-three-quarter millions of pounds per annum: new taxes in defiance of the Act had been imposed: Ireland, again in defiance of the Act, had been made jointly responsible for a debt which was not her own: Irish banks and Irish railways were managed not with reference to Irish interests but in the interests of English finance and English trade: the Irish mercantile marine was no more: the mineral resources of the country in coal and iron remained undeveloped lest their development might act unfavourably upon vested interests in Great Britain. The population had declined at a rate without parallel in Europe: even Ulster, proclaimed to be prosperous because Protestant and Unionist, had seen the population of its most "loyal" counties almost halved in the space of seventy years. Nothing but the removal of the cause could arrest this spreading decay, and the cause was declared to be irremovable: to tamper with it was to lay an impious hand upon the Ark of a grim Covenant.

But the last refuge of independence was still safe—resolve was still strong—no weakness of acquiescence, no dimness of spirit, no decay of the soul was as yet to be discerned? An answer to these questions might be found in the history of the language and of what the possession of a native language implied. Up to the time of the Union the Gaelic language had preserved intact, in spite of Penal Laws and the instruments of repression, all that was most vital in the national spirit. Tales of warriors and heroes, of the long wars of the Gael with the stranger, the sighs of love and the aspirations of devotion, satire and encomium, all the literature and song of a people were enshrined in the native tongue. Behind it, as behind an unassailable rampart, the national culture was preserved, in misery and degradation, it is true, the mere shadow of what it was and might be, but still its existence was secure. The Irish language was understood all over Ireland, and was the familiar tongue of three-quarters of its inhabitants. It was not a necessary consequence of the Union itself that this should be destroyed, but it was a necessary consequence of the measures which the Act of Union made it possible to take. The English Government decided to embark upon the task of " civilizing" the inhabitants of Ireland by a comprehensive system of practical education. In 1831 the " National " Education system was founded and before the century was old its work was done: it had " educated " Ireland out of its traditional civilization and culture. The authors and administrators of this system were sincere and well-intentioned men: they believed that they were removing a disability and conferring a benefit. They regarded ignorance as barbarous and disgraceful; and what was ignorance if it was not inability to write, read, and speak the English tongue? A love of learning had always distinguished the Irish people; and here was the learning, for which so many vain sacrifices had been made in the past, brought in full measure to their very doors. Everything that might induce suspicion of the Danai, *dona ferentes*, was carefully avoided. The Catholic Archbishop of Dublin held a seat on the Board and no book was sanctioned by the Board without his unreserved acquiescence. The Catholic clergy were encouraged to take a share in the administration of the schools and to supervise or impart the religious instruction of the pupils. It was the avowed policy of the Board to avoid anything that might savour of proselytism on the one hand and of the perpetuation of sectarian discord on the other. Pupils of the two creeds were to meet together on equal terms and in friendly rivalry in the classroom, while their particular religious interests were entrusted to their respective clergy. But this paternal care for the susceptibilities of Irish children, this careful abhorrence of sectarian animosities, went hand in hand with an elaborate disregard of every distinctive national feeling and characteristic. English was the language of the school, while Irish was the language of the fireside and of the street. Irish history was ignored: references to national and patriotic sentiments were carefully excluded, as a possible disturbing influence, from the approved text books: while the privilege of being "British," and the duty of feeling it to be a privilege, were carefully inculcated.

It may seem extraordinary that such a system should have been accepted, even if the attempt to impose it were made. But in fact the bribe of knowledge is a great bribe; and in this case the consequence of taking it was in obscurity. To learn English was to possess the only key to the knowledge that was offered, and when English was learnt, the language of "progress" crushed the language of tradition. A few far-seeing Irishmen, like Archbishop MacHale,, saw the inevitable tendency and endeavoured to correct it; but in general no one noticed that the Irish language was going until everyone noticed that it had gone. Men's minds were set upon other things. The struggle for political independence and political and social equality absorbed energy and attention, and the political struggle had to be carried on by men who understood English. O'Connell's election for the county of Clare struck a deadly blow at the preservation of the language and at all that the preservation of the language implied: he himself, with a miserable servility, refused to speak any tongue but the tongue of Parliament. The National Board of Education did not, it is true, escape criticism: but the criticism was directed not to its educational shortcomings or to its antinational bias, but to its policy of "religious indifference." The Presbyterian ministers were up in arms against a system by which "the Gospel" was excluded from the schools. They claimed the right to conduct the schools supported by the Board in defiance of the terms upon which the Board had promised to support them. They contended for the principle of a programme in which the reading of the Bible might at any moment without notice be substituted by a Presbyterian teacher for any item on the programme for the day, any Catholic children who happened to be in attendance being allowed to withdraw, the responsibility for the child's spiritual loss being solemnly laid upon the shoulders of the parents. The Protestant clergy, who were supposed as part of their duty to keep schools in their parishes, though they had neglected the duty for generations, followed with similar claims. They stirred up their congregations until mobs took to wrecking the National Schools in counties like Antrim and Down, and rifle clubs were formed under the patronage of the local aristocracy for the defence of their threatened Bibles. Under the Ultramontane leadership of Cardinal Cullen the Catholic clergy adopted a similar attitude. They alleged that the National system was hostile to their faith. Whatever danger to the faith had been contained in it had at any rate escaped the vigilance of Archbishop Murray and the authorities whom he had consulted. But the spirit of religious animosity once let loose could not be chained; and the system which began by promoting the co-education of the two creeds, ended by a segregating of the population from infancy into hostile camps. This accomplished the end which was designed by nobody but reached by everybody, that of breaking down the feeling of national unity and perpetuating feelings which it had been the aim of patriots to obliterate.

But though the closing decade of the nineteenth century presented a spectacle of national disunion and apathy, of failing vigour and vanishing ideals, it saw the beginning of a movement destined to arrest the decline of one department of the national life. The foundation of the Gaelic League in 1893 may be regarded as the turning point in the history of the language. When it was on the verge of extinction its decline was stayed by the enthusiastic patriotism of Dr. Douglas Hyde. Non-political and non-sectarian, the League worked for the restoration, preservation and diffusion of the Irish language, Irish music and Irish industries. In its councils Catholic priests and laymen worked side by side with Protestant laymen and ministers. It not only revived the language (its first and main object) but it proved incidentally, as if in answer to a frequent but foolish criticism, that Irishmen of different creeds and political opinions could sink their differences in the common interests of patriotism. It kept rigidly and sternly aloof from all connection with professedly political parties. It had no more to do with official Nationalism than it had to do with Ulster Unionism. It resisted with success the attempts of some of the clergy to interfere with its programme: in the case of the parish priest of Portarlington who objected to mixed classes on the specious ground of public morals it asserted its rights to control its own activities and established once for all, so far as it was concerned, the principle that the sphere of the clergy's activities is not co-extensive with human life. It criticized the Hierarchy with as much independence as it would have criticized a local Board of Guardians; and in the end it won and held the enthusiastic support of the best elements in Irish life. Looking from things temporal and devoting itself to things of the mind, it widened the horizon and cleared the outlook of many districts through all Ireland. P. H. Pearse said with truth " The Gaelic League will be recognized in history as the most revolutionary influence that ever came into Ireland." The revolution which it wrought was moral, intellectual and spiritual and its influence in strengthening and developing the national character can hardly be over-estimated. Blamed alike for doing too much and for not doing enough, it adhered with undeviating consistency to its own programme and has been fully justified by its work. It stimulated activities in spheres far remote from its own. It enriched Anglo-Irish literature through the works of writers to whom it opened a new field and for whom it provided a fresh stimulus. There is hardly a writer in Ireland to-day of any promise in either prose or verse who does not owe a heavy debt to the work of the Gaelic League.

The Gaelic League proceeded upon the assumption that Irishmen possessed and ought to possess an interest in the language of their own country. It did not argue the point or indulge in academic discussions upon the utility of Gaelic as a medium of communication or upon the psychology of language. Its simple appeal to a natural human feeling found a response wider than could have been evoked by a learned controversy or effected as the fruit of a dialectical victory. But language is only a part of nationality and the attachment of a human being to the language of his country is only a special case of his attachment to the nation. This, though the Gaelic League held aloof from all politics (in the narrow sense of the word), is what gave to the work of the Gaelic League a real political importance. The stimulation of national sentiment in one department gave a stimulus to the same sentiment in other departments, and the new and vigorous national sense which it fostered was bound to lead sooner or later to expression in political action. But even after this political activity began to be manifest, the League confined itself to its original work, and held as much aloof from politics infused by its own spirit as from the forms of political action which held the field when its work began.

Sinn Fein is an expression in political theory and action of the claim of Ireland to be a nation, with all the practical consequences which such a claim involves. It differs from previous national movements principally in the policy which it outlines for the attainment of its ultimate end, the independence of Ireland: though it should be understood that nearly every point in the Sinn Fein political programme had been at least suggested by some previous Irish Nationalist thinker. In opposition to the Parliamentary Party it held that for Ireland to send representatives to Westminster was to acknowledge the validity of the Act of Union and virtually to deny the Irish claim to an independent legislature. In contrast with the National movements of '48 and '67 it disclaimed the use of physical force for the attainment of its ends. While it held as a matter of abstract political ethics that a nation subjugated against its will by another nation is justified in regaining its independence, if it can do so, by any means at its disposal, including force, yet as a matter of practical Irish politics it renounced the use of force unequivocally. " It is because Ireland is to-day unable to overcome England on the battlefield we preach the Sinn Fein policy," wrote the principal exponent of the policy in 1906. The remnants of the Fenian Brotherhood had no sympathy with a policy such as this: and though representatives of the " physical force party " were allowed to express their opinions in the Sinn Fein papers, their views were not officially adopted and never became part of the Sinn Fein policy. At least one prominent member of the old Fenian Party saw reason to adopt the Sinn Fein policy in preference to that of armed force. " I would not," wrote John Devoy from New York in 1911, "incite the unorganized, undisciplined and unarmed people of Ireland to a hopeless military struggle with England." This renunciation of force was however very different from O'Connell's famous declaration of his intention not to fight. While Sinn Fein held that the most practical way to establish Irish freedom in the twentieth century was not the way of force it never concealed its opinion that force was a legitimate method of securing national rights. In fact no responsible national leader has ever held any other opinion in any country.

Nor was the Sinn Fein Party in its inception a Republican Party. It was strictly constitutional, and in fact forfeited the support of many ardent

Nationalists by adherence to this definitely constitutional policy. While the Parliamentary Party claimed to be the only constitutional party by its use of the forms of the existing constitution, Sinn Fein laid claim to the merit of a superior constitutionalism. It relied upon the Renunciation Act of 1783 which declared that the right "claimed by the people of Ireland to be bound only by laws enacted by his Majesty and the Parliament of that kingdom, in all cases whatever, and to have all actions and suits at law or in equity which may be instituted in that kingdom decided in his Majesty's courts therein finally and without appeal from thence shall be and it is hereby declared to be established and ascertained forever and shall at no time hereafter be questioned or questionable." The Act of Union, carried as it was, was a clear breach of this declaration, and the policy of Sinn Fein was to ignore, holding it as null and void, the Union and every subsequent arrangement made in contravention of the Act of 1783. If it came to a question of constitutionalism Sinn Fein took up a High Tory attitude compared with the accommodating constitutionalism of the official Nationalist Party.

Though Sinn Fein as a political organization in being did not exist till 1905 the way had been smoothed for it and several actual steps taken several years before. The first symptom of the coming movement was the establishment of literary societies which drew their inspiration from the Young Ireland movement of the 'forties, and the publication in Belfast by Miss Alice Milligan of the *Shan Van Vocht*, a literary and political journal which became a semi-official exponent of the new Irish-Ireland movement. The centenary celebration of the Rebellion of 1798 led to a quickening of interest in the history of Irish separatist movements and an endeavour was made to keep the interest from dying out by the establishment of '98 Clubs. Finally in 1899 the *United Irishman* was founded by Mr. Arthur Griffith.

The title which Mr. Griffith chose for his paper is significant. The adoption of the name of John Mitchel's paper was more than a hint that John Mitchel's policy was to be revived. But it was to be the policy, not of the abortive revolution of '48, but that expressed earlier in a prescient passage. A plan (said Mitchel) for the repeal of the Union " must develop not one sole plan followed out to the end, but three or four of the possible and probable series of events which may evidently lead to the result. It must show (for one way) how a parliamentary campaign, conducted honestly and boldly, might bring the state of public business in Parliament to such a position that repeal would be the only solution; for another way, how systematic passive opposition to, and contempt of, *law* might be carried out through a thousand details, so as to virtually supersede English dominion here and to make the mere repealing statute an immaterial formality (this, I may observe, is *my* way); and for a third way how, in the event of an European war, a strong national party in Ireland could grasp the occasion to do the work instantly . . . . It should also show how and to what extent all these methods of operation might be combined." In this one passage Mitchel sketched successively the Parnell policy, the Sinn Fein policy and the policy of the Easter Rising.

*The United Irishman* ran as a weekly paper from March 4, 1899, to April 14, 1906. During this time twenty-three issues were seized and confiscated in the Post Office and upon three occasions in the year 1900 the paper was publicly suppressed. In 1905 the Secret Service threatened the printer with prosecution unless the printing of the paper was discontinued; and in 1906 the increasing liabilities of the United Irishman Publishing Company (who engaged Mr. Griffith as editor) led to the discontinuance of the paper. But before it ceased publication the Sinn Fein Movement had been successfully inaugurated. The paper was remarkable for the ability with which it was edited, the literary excellence of its articles both editorial and contributed, the range of its topics and the freedom which it allowed to the discussion in its columns of different views. Its contributors included many of the best-known Irish writers, though many of them were not (or did not remain) in sympathy with its political propaganda. It championed the cause of the Gaelic League, of native industries, of native music and of native games. It spread information upon the mineral resources of Ireland, its waterways, its railways, its vital statistics, and the menace of emigration. It republished as serials such standard works as John Mitchel's *Apology* and an authorized translation of D'Arbois de Jubainville's *Irish Mythological Cycle*. Mr. Best contributed a series of articles on "The Old Irish Bardic Tales." It published a drama by W. B. Yeats and its columns were always open to literary and dramatic criticisms and discussions. It had a weekly column on European politics. And finally it argued with courage, brilliancy and passion the cause of Irish independence.

The editorial in the first number gives a general idea both of the style and of the teaching of the paper. " There exists, has existed for centuries, and will continue to exist in Ireland, a conviction hostile to the subjection, or dependence of the fortunes of this country to the necessities of any other; we intend to voice that conviction. We bear no ill will to any section of the Irish political body, whether its flag be green or orange, which holds that tortuous paths are the safest for Irishmen to tread; but, knowing we are governed by a nation which religiously adheres to ' The good old rule—the simple plan—that those may take who have the power, and those may keep who can,' we, with all respect for our friends who love the devious ways, are convinced that an occasional exhibition of the naked truth will not shock the modesty of Irishmen and that a return to the straight road will not lead us to political destruction . . . . To be perfectly plain, we believe that when Swift wrote to the whole people of Ireland 170 years ago, that by the law of God, of Nature, and of nations they had a right to be as free a people as the people of England, he wrote commonsense; notwithstanding that in these latter days we have been diligently taught that by the law of God, of Nature, and of nations we are rightfully entitled to the establishment in Dublin of a legislative assembly with an expunging angel watching over its actions from the Viceregal Lodge. We do not deprecate the institution of any such body, but we do assert that the whole duty of an Irishman is not comprised in utilizing all the forces of his nature to procure its inception . . . . With the present day Irish movements outside politics we are in more or less sympathy. The Financial Reformers . . . . are incidentally doing good in promoting an union of Irishmen in opposition to their one enemy; the resuscitation of our national language is a work in which everyone of us should help; at the same time we would regret any insistence on a knowledge of Gaelic as a test of patriotism. It is scarcely necessary to say we are in full sympathy with the objects of the Amnesty Association; but we shall not at any time support an appeal to any such myths as English Justice or English Mercy . . . . Lest there might be any doubt in any mind we will say that we accept the Nationalism of '98, '48 and '67 as the true Nationalism and Grattan's cry ' Live Ireland—Perish the Empire !' as the watchword of patriotism."

The political creed of the *United Irishman* was the absolute independence of Ireland; and though it did not advocate the methods of armed revolution it opened its columns to those Nationalists who did: though its policy was the re-establishment of the Constitution of 1782, not the establishment of an Irish Republic, it contained articles written by Republicans who made no secret of their views. But the object of this, confusing to the careless or intermittent reader, was gradually to build up a kind of national forum in which all "real" Nationalists might have their say, and to induce a general consensus of opinion in favour of the new policy. Its aim at first was strictly critical and educational. In writing of the '98 Clubs the editor says: "We look to them for the fostering of a national and tolerant public opinion, which will raise the *morale* of the people, so grievously lowered by the squalid agitations of the past; we look to them for the inculcation of the doctrine of self-reliance, without which neither our land nor any other can hope for salvation; and we look to them anxiously for the teaching and training of youth, for our future depends largely on the young." Everything was made to turn upon the question of self-reliance and independence: what inculcated or enhanced these qualities was good, what hindered them was bad or (at best) indifferent. Political independence was regarded as the sequel and corollary of moral independence, and all political action that sacrificed this stood self-condemned. Under this condemnation fell

in the first place the Irish Parliamentary Party: their policy was derided as one of "half-bluster and half-whine": when Mr. Redmond spoke, in an unguarded moment, of "wringing from whatever Government may be in power the full measure of a nation's rights" he was bluntly told that all this was "arrant humbug." "After one hundred years of the British Parliament we are poorer and fewer, and our taxation has been multiplied by ten. All the signs of the times point to the continuance of this policy of practically burning the candle at both ends; and our self-respect and our status before the nations of Europe would be infinitely raised by a manly refusal to lend the support of our presence to an assembly in which our interests are ignored whenever they clash, and sometimes when they do not clash, with the interests of England. If our 'Parliamentary representatives' had spirit, they would have retired from the British Parliament when the Home Rule Bill was defeated, and have told their constituents that they were wasting time in fighting Ireland's battle with British weapons and that further representation at Westminster was 'neither possible nor desirable.' That would have been a protest that would have roused the attention of the civilized world and even now it would be well that such a protest should be made; for it *is* waste of time and money and a source of degradation to countenance a system which ignores us.
. . . . . By turning their attention to the practical development of industries in Ireland and

pledging themselves to a policy of practical support and preference for the products of Irish labour, our people can undoubtedly advance the social condition and prosperity of the country; but while they are hoping against hope for some vague indefinite assistance from Westminster, a genuine manly effort in this direction is impossible."

If the Parliamentary Party was charged with futility and lack of dignity, other Irish movements were criticized with a similar candour. Even the Gaelic League did not win the entire and unqualified approval of the national Mentor. The " persistent labouring of the fact that the language question is non-political" was held to savour of a certain lack of candour and of courage. The Gaelic movement (it was said) had for its aim " the intensifying of Irish sentiment, the preservation of Irish ideals": it aroused enthusiasm " by awakening memories hot with hate and fierce with desire of vengeance on the foreigner." It was asserted that " as a factor towards freedom, and as such *alone*, the people will respond to its claims upon them: for them culture has no charms"; and the League was bluntly told that it could not continue to pursue its policy of aloofness. " With politics," wrote William Rooney (who seems to have held a unique position of authority and trust in the new movement up to the time of his early death), " as at present understood, and which, after all, mean nothing but partisanship, the Gaelic League has rightly had nothing to do; but with politics, in the sense of some public policy aiming at the reincarnation of an Irish nation, it cannot refuse to meddle." The Gaelic League, like the Parliamentary Party, pursued its way undisturbed: but the criticism was not unmarked. And the Catholic clergy (so often represented as immune from the criticism of all good Irish Nationalists) were faithfully (and not always tenderly) taken to task when they wandered from the straight path; it was said that they took no effective steps to arrest emigration: that they "next to the British Government" were " responsible for the depopulation of the country": that they failed to encourage Irish trade and manufactures: that the priests " made life dull and unendurable for the people": that the Hierarchy had backed the Parliamentary Party against the Nationalists of '48 and '67: that they were apathetic on the question of the language. It was asserted that the priesthood with their exaggerated caution with regard to the natural relations of the sexes had " brought a Calvinistic gloom and horror into Ireland"; "To-day the land is dotted with religious edifices but the men and women whose money built them are fleeing to America to seek for bread." " It is high time this monstrous hypocrisy should be faced and fought. While the country is making a last fight for existence its people are being bled right and left to build all kinds of church edifices and endow all kinds of church institutions and their money is being sent abroad to England, Italy, and Germany. . . . . We strongly advise the Irish people not to subscribe a single penny in future towards the eternal church building funds unless they first receive public assurances that their money will be expended in Ireland." These criticisms are characteristic of the candour and consistency with which the test was applied to all movements, bodies and institutions in Ireland: were they or were they not a factor in the material and moral upbuilding of the Irish nation as a free and self-reliant community.

The war against the Transvaal Republics made the question of recruiting for the army a question of public importance in Ireland during the early days of the paper, and its articles on the subject first brought it into conflict with the Castle authorities. That Mr. Chamberlain's policy was directed to the extinction of Transvaal independence was self-evident and the war on that account was not popular in Ireland. In the Boers struggling hopelessly for the maintenance of their freedom was seen an analogue of the long Irish struggle for independence, and any Irishman who enlisted in the British army was denounced as " a traitor to his country and a felon in his soul." But it was not the crushing of Transvaal independence in which the army was employed that formed the only argument against enlisting. The official returns of the statistics of venereal disease in the British army were printed with a commentary of provoking frankness. The excesses of the British army in Burmah and the charges made against the soldiers for offences against

Burmese women were insisted upon to prove that no decent Irishman could join the army. But in fact it was something more than the sufferings of the Boers and the Burmese which inspired this attitude. The British army was regarded as the instrument by which Ireland was held in subjugation, as the force which upheld the power to whose interests Ireland was sacrificed. One of the concluding numbers of the paper printed the text of an anti-recruiting pamphlet for the distribution of which prosecutions were instituted. It concluded: " Let England fight her own battles: we have done it long enough. Let her arm and drill the sickly population of her slums: the men of the hills and country places in Ireland will go no more. Let her fight for the extension of her Empire herself, for the men of the Gael are not going to be bribed into betraying themselves and their country again at the bidding of England." It was found difficult to obtain convictions against persons who distributed these pamphlets. Even in Belfast a jury refused to convict a man for this at the instance of the Crown: though the accused made no excuse or apology, and though his counsel said in his speech to the jury, " You are fathers and brothers, and there is not one of you who would not rather see your boys in hell than in the British Army."

The seizure of the *United Irishman* by order of Lord Cadogan in consequence of its anti-recruiting propaganda served only to advertise its attitude, and secure for it some of the popularity which attends whatever is in conflict with the authorities in Ireland. It also urged the paper to further efforts in the same direction and from the time of Queen Victoria's visit in 1900, " who now in her dotage," as the leader on the subject ran, " is sent amongst us to seek recruits for her battered army," it was in constant conflict with the Irish police.

While the *United Irishman* pursued its extensive and boisterous business, of which this full account is significant and pertinent, an organization of Irishmen who shared its views generally was being slowly formed. In one of the early numbers of the paper a contributed article on "A National Organization" had appeared (and been approved of in a leader), urging the formation of a party " with the openly avowed and ultimate object of ending British rule" in Ireland; such an organization should honestly acknowledge " its present inability to lead Ireland to victory against the armed might of her enemy" and confine itself "for some time to the disciplining of the mind and the training of the forces of the nation, whilst impressing on it that, in the last resort, nothing save the weapons of freemen can regain its independence . . . . It need have no secrecy about it whatsoever . . . . Such an organization should . . . . require only two qualifications from its members, one, that they declare themselves advocates of an Irish Republic, the other, that they be persons of decent character . . . . It should adopt no attitude of

antagonism to the Parliamentarians; but point
out to the people that Parliamentarianism is not
Nationalism, and leave them, in their own judgment, to give it what support they pleased.
Toleration, free impersonal criticism, and sympathy with every man seeking, after his own light,
the welfare of our common country, should be
distinguishing characteristics of the organization
and its members." Discussion of these proposals,
partly favourable, partly critical, followed and in
October, 1900, the first steps were taken in the
foundation of the Cumann na nGaedhal. Its
objects were to advance the cause of Ireland's
national independence by (1) cultivating a
fraternal spirit amongst Irishmen; (2) diffusing
knowledge of Ireland's resources and supporting
Irish industries; (3) the study and teaching of
Irish history, literature, language, music and art;
(4) the assiduous cultivation and encouragement
of Irish games, pastimes and characteristics; (5)
the discountenancing of anything tending towards
the anglicization of Ireland; (6) the physical and
intellectual training of the young; (7) the development of an Irish foreign policy; (8) extending to
each other friendly advice and aid, socially and
politically; (9) the nationalization of public
boards. Membership was open to "all persons of
Irish birth or descent undertaking to obey its
rules, carry out its constitution, and pledging
themselves to aid to the best of their ability in
restoring Ireland to her former position of
sovereign independence." The *United Irishman*

commenting on this observes: " It comes to interfere with no policy before the people—it asks only the help and support of Irish Nationalists . . . Let us be Irish in act and speech, as we pretend to be in heart and spirit, and a few years will prove whether the remedy is not better sought at home among ourselves than beyond the waters." While the association aimed at the cultivation of a spirit of self-reliance and the attainment of a moral independence, it was clear that the realization of its ideals would be a slow process and would leave the actual political situation much as it was. The whole Irish nation might talk Irish, play Irish games, support Irish industries, deanglicize their children, have their own ideas of foreign policy and love one another like brothers, and yet Ireland would not have regained independence. The ends of Cumann na nGaedhal were remote and, if attained, unsatisfactory to those to whom independence meant more than a mere lofty disregard of the truth that Ireland was as a matter of fact politically dependent on another country. Something more was needed to bring the new policy (if it could be called new) into more intimate connection with political facts. The link with current politics was supplied by Mr. Griffith in an address which he gave to the third annual convention of Cumann na nGaedhal in October, 1902, in which he outlined what came to be known afterwards as the Hungarian Policy. The new policy, instead of adopting a neutral attitude towards existing political parties in Ireland, boldly declared war upon the Irish Parliamentary Party. The Convention passed the following resolution: " That we call upon our countrymen abroad to withhold all assistance from the promoters of a useless, degrading and demoralizing policy until such times as the members of the Irish Parliamentary Party substitute for it the policy of the Hungarian Deputies of 1861, and, refusing to attend the British Parliament or to recognize its right to legislate for Ireland, remain at home to help in promoting Ireland's interests and to aid in guarding its national rights." With this resolution Sinn Fein may be said to have been inaugurated.

Though the policy of abstention from Parliament came to be known as " the Hungarian Policy" it was a policy that had been advocated, and to a certain extent practised, in Ireland long before the Hungarian Deputies adopted it. In 1844, the " Parliamentary Committee of the Loyal National Repeal Association on the Attendance of Irish Members in Parliament" presented a report which contained the following: " The people of Ireland, having in vain attempted to obtain from the Imperial Parliament detailed measures of justice, and with equal failure sought the restoration of their domestic Senate or even inquiry into the wisdom of that restoration, have at length sought to obtain those rights by agitation out of Parliament. They have to this end arrayed themselves into a Loyal and National Association to obtain the Repeal of the Union. They try to obtain strength by the reality and display of union

SINN FEIN 67

and organization. They seek converts by their speeches, their writings, and their peaceful virtues. They are endeavouring to increase their knowledge and their power by reading, thinking and discussing. And to carry out their projects of organization, conversion and self-improvement, they subscribe large funds to a common treasury. Their efforts in the Imperial Parliament having then been so fruitless, and their undertaking at home being so vast, they, the people of Ireland, have consented that such of their members as seek with them domestic legislation, should secede from the Imperial Parliament and control the agitation, instruction and organization of the people at home." This report is signed by Thomas Davis. A correspondence between Thomas Davis and the Earl of Wicklow, to whom certain resolutions of the Repeal Association had been sent, debates the rival merits of the policies of parliamentarianism and abstention. The Earl, who had no intention of leaving Parliament, wrote: " I now believe that there exists amongst the British people an anxious desire to do justice to our country and to atone in every way in their power for the evils of former mismanagement." Lord Wicklow had formed this conviction before 1844. The "Hungarian Policy" of 1902 was framed for the same situation and in face of the same conviction.

It is difficult to understand why the credit of the policy was not claimed for Thomas Davis the Irishman instead of for the Hungarian Franz Deák:

unless it be that the policy had in the case of Ireland never been put into actual effective practice and had remained fruitless of result, while in Hungary it had seemed to have achieved its object. Be that as it may, Mr. Arthur Griffith proceeded to contribute to the *United Irishman* a series of articles on "The Resurrection of Hungary," reprinted in book form the same year and widely circulated. The preface represented the policy as an alternative to that of armed resistance: the body of the book gave a historical account of the struggle of the Hungarians under Deák for the restoration of the constitution of 1848 and its success, due (it was claimed) entirely to Deák's policy of abstention from the Austrian Imperial Parliament: the concluding chapter drew the parallel between Hungary and Ireland, claiming that by abstaining from sending members to Westminster Ireland could secure the restoration of the constitution of 1782. The book was interesting and able: the narrative was presented with vigour and spirit: but the accuracy of some of its statements and conclusions was open to question and as a piece of popular propaganda it was a failure. While many people read it, it produced no immediate or widespread response. Exception was taken to the view that Ireland ought to aim at the restoration of the constitution of 1782: exception was taken to the substitution of a peaceful for a forcible policy. "If the Irish members" (wrote a representative of the latter body of critics) "of the English Parliament withdrew from Westminster to-morrow

the government of the country would be carried on
just as it is to-day; and so it will and must be as
long as the people forget they are Irishmen with
a country to free from a foreign yoke. The protest would end in smoke unless armed men were
prepared to back it."

Mr. Griffith, nothing daunted, continued his
fight against on the one hand the traditional parliamentarianism and on the other hand the advocates of physical force and revolution and the
members of the Republican Party. His claim to
independence for Ireland was to be based not upon
force but upon law and the constitution of 1782:
his claim was not a Republic but a national constitution under an Irish Crown. He tried to show
in a series of articles on "The Working of the
Policy"—which from now on begins to be referred
to as the Sinn Fein Policy—how his ideas might be
put into practice. But to carry on such a policy
as he had outlined, some political organization
other than the Cumann na nGaedhael or the '98
Clubs was required. This was inaugurated at a
meeting held in Dublin on November 28th, 1905,
under the chairmanship of Mr. Edward Martyn.
The policy of the new body, the National Council,
was defined as "National self-development through
the recognition of the rights and duties of citizenship on the part of the individual and by the aid
and support of all movements originating from
within Ireland, instinct with national tradition
and not looking outside Ireland for the accomplishment of their aims." A public meeting held after-

wards in the Rotunda passed the following resolution: " That the people of Ireland are a free people and that no law made without their authority and consent is or can ever be binding on their conscience. That the General Council of County Councils presents the nucleus of a national authority, and we urge upon it to extend the scope of its deliberation and action: to take within its purview every question of national interest and to formulate lines of procedure for the nation." Mr. Griffith, who was the main-spring and driving force of the movement, speaking in favour of the resolution, proposed the formation of a council of 300 to sit in Dublin and form a *de facto* Irish Parliament, with whom might be associated all those members of Parliament who refused to attend at Westminster; its recommendations should be binding upon all County Councils and Boards of Guardians, whose duty it would be to carry them into effect as far as their powers extended.

With this meeting ends the preliminary stage, and Sinn Fein formally takes its place as a duly constituted political party with its own policy and aims. The *United Irishman*, the organ of its infancy, ceased to exist, and its place was taken by *Sinn Fein*.

## THE EARLY YEARS OF SINN FEIN.

In the year 1906 Sinn Fein emerged from the region of ideals and abstractions, of academical discussion and preliminary propaganda, into the arena of Irish party politics with a fully formulated practical policy. Taking constitutional ground with the dictum that " the constitution of 1782 is still the constitution of Ireland," it proposed to show how the people of Ireland, keeping within the letter of a law which they could not otherwise break, might render nugatory the effort to hold the country in dependence upon England in pursuance of the Act of Union. It proposed to arrest the anglicization of Ireland by recovering for the Irish people the management of those departments of public administration in which the anglicizing process was working most markedly to the detriment of Irish interests and which might be remodelled without any actual breach of the existing law. In the first place it seemed necessary to take education in hand, and by the introduction of a system more in accordance with Irish needs and capabilities and characteristics, endeavour to train up a generation of young Irish men and women, imbued with a national spirit and national pride, capable of taking their part in the agricultural, industrial and administrative life of the country. County Councils might do much in this direction through their intimate connection with the administration and policy of the Department of Agriculture and Technical Instruction; a wise use of the means placed by the Department at their disposal might in a few years revolutionize to the advantage of Ireland the entire education of the country. The young men and women thus trained might form the nucleus of an Irish Civil Service, if the County Councils could be induced to abandon their "patronage" in the positions at their disposal and throw them open to competitive examination; others of these trained Irishmen might be employed in an unofficial Irish Consular Service to the great advantage of Irish commerce, handicapped in foreign markets by English consuls in the interests of the English commercial houses. Pressure could be brought to bear upon the Irish banks to adopt a policy more in sympathy with Irish trade and industry. There was deposited in Irish banks a sum of £50,000,000, the savings of the people of Ireland; yet these banks invested this money in English securities (the Bank of Ireland during the South African War even lent money to the English Government without interest) while Irish industries were starving for lack of the capital which the banks refused to lend. The Stock Exchange, controlled by the Government, neglected to quote shares in Irish companies that might be formed for the furtherance of particular industries in particular districts, discouraging investors who were thus left unable to dispose of their shares in the ordinary way. It was hoped that public bodies as well as private persons could be induced to bring pressure to bear on the banks by withdrawing or withholding accounts until they should adopt a more patriotic policy, though it was more difficult to see how the Stock Exchange could be dealt with. The difficulties put by railways and their heavy freights on the exchange of commodities could be obviated by a development of the Irish waterways under the control of popularly elected bodies: the County Councils should see to this and to questions such as afforestation and the encouragement of home manufactures by specifying their use in the giving of contracts for institutions under their control. The Poor Law system should be remodelled in accordance with Irish sentiment and the money expended upon it spent in Ireland upon Irish goods. To ensure the advantage of foreign markets without English interference an Irish Mercantile Marine should be established, what could be done even by a poor country in this way being shown by the example of Norway, where nearly everyone was at least part owner of a ship.

But to stimulate and foster native industry and native manufacture was to Mr. Griffith (whose writings on economic matters formed a kind of gospel for Sinn Fein) an urgent and supreme duty. He was convinced that until Ireland became an industrial as well as an agricultural country her economic position was insecure. Thinking always in terms of national independence, which he inter-

preted to mean national ability to dispense with
outside assistance, he looked forward to a time
when Ireland should be able not merely to feed
her population from her own resources, but to
supply them with nearly all the other necessaries
of modern life. Irish coal and iron existed in
abundance to supply the necessary fuel and raw
material; there was plenty of native marble and
other stones for building; Irish wool and hides
were once famous over Europe for their abundance and excellence. All that was required to
make Ireland once more a prosperous manufacturing country was at her disposal within her own
boundaries, and only waited for the policy that
would call out her latent powers. In an independent State the encouragement required would be
forthcoming in protective legislation, pursued
until the protected industry became established
and able to compete on favourable terms with
similar industries in other countries, the work of
protection being limited strictly to the task of
building up a temporary screen to shelter a bud-
ding national industry from the wind of competi-
tion until its strength was established. The Irish
Parliament in the days of its independence had
adopted this policy, which had enabled it during
its short life to secure to Irish manufactures an unprecedented prosperity. But Ireland, deprived of
legislative powers, might fall back upon a less
secure but still efficacious method of protection.
Irish consumers might refuse to purchase English
goods while Irish goods of the same quality were

to be had, and be content to pay in an enhanced price their share of what under other circumstances the State might have expended in bounties to the industry; public bodies might insist upon the use of goods of Irish manufacture; port authorities should arrange port dues so that they should fall most heavily on manufactured goods brought into the country, and should publish periodical returns of the imports of manufactured goods at every port in Ireland; Irish capital should be invited and encouraged to undertake the development of the country on industrial and commercial lines, being assured, in the support of industrial and corporate public feeling, of encouragement and success in its enterprise.

In expounding this theory of protection and of the vital necessity to a country of developing its industrial life Mr. Griffith was confessedly following the economic doctrines of the German economist Friedrich List, "the man whom England caused to be persecuted by the Government of his native country, and whom she hated and feared more than any man since Napoleon—the man who saved Germany from falling a prey to English economics, and whose brain conceived the great industrial and economic Germany of to-day." A man with credentials like these might well be listened to with profit. The commercial policy that made the New Germany could not fail to make a New Ireland, and List made seductive promises. He foretold an increase in population by a combination of agricultural and industrial enterprise greater in proportion than by the development of either industry or agriculture by itself: he denied the possibility of intellectual progress to a country relying solely or mainly upon agriculture: culture marched behind the mill and the factory. But the chief merit of the policy undoubtedly was that it promised a self-contained and independent economic existence, serving as the basis of a distinctive national culture.

The merits of List's theories in the abstract it is for economists to determine: but the concrete instance of the commercial expansion of Germany seemed at the time a sufficient vindication of their merit. But Germany was an independent State, competent to fix its own tariffs, give State encouragement to its industries and determine its own destinies. Ireland could do none of these things: the efforts of individuals, societies and local bodies would have to supply the place of legislative control, their efforts must be voluntary and would be difficult to control and co-ordinate. To ensure the will to follow out the suggested policy if it were even accepted, and to secure its acceptance, was a work of argument and controversy, and to secure a sympathetic or even attentive audience was not easy. Great claims were made upon the national intelligence and the national conscience, and success could only be ensured by practical unanimity. Unanimity was not to be had, and could hardly be expected in the near future: the task of securing it was one to tax the resources of a generation of apostles, in the absence of some

cataclysm which might involve a complete change
in the general outlook and ensure the acceptance
of the policy by the mere force of circumstances.
Meanwhile something might be done to co-ordinate
spasmodic and voluntary effort. In the absence
of a Parliament it might be possible to bring together a representative assembly whose directions
and decisions might carry a moral sanction to the
conscience of an awakened public and to this end
it was proposed to constitute a Council of Three
Hundred, forming a *de facto* Irish Parliament. A
similar council had been suggested by O'Connell,
prolific of expedients: but, sterile in execution,
he had never permitted it to meet and transact
business. The expedient was now to be revived:
the Council was, upon report from special committees (such as those that had been appointed by
the Repeal Association) " to deliberate and formulate workable schemes, which, once formulated,
it would be the duty of all County and Urban
Councils, Rural Councils, Poor Law Boards, and
other bodies to give legal effect to so far as their
powers permit, and where these legal powers fell
short, to give it the moral force of law by instruct-
ing and inducing those whom they represent to
honour and obey the recommendations of the
Council of Three Hundred, individually and collectively." Finally, Arbitration Courts were to
be instituted to supersede the ordinary courts of
law in civil cases, which " would deprive the cor-
rupt bar of Ireland of much of its incentive to
corruption" and foster a spirit of brotherhood.

Such was the new policy: and it was claimed that " not on recognition of usurped authority, but on its denial—not on aid from our enemies but on action for ourselves, the Sinn Fein policy is based. Its essence is construction and its march to its ultimate political goal must be attended at every step by the material progress of the nation." The work of exposition and instruction was carried on partly in the columns of *Sinn Fein* partly by means of clubs and branches through the country. A branch was formed in Belfast in the early autumn of 1906, and at the meeting of the National Council a month later it was announced that there were already twenty branches in existence. At that meeting resolutions were passed in favour of boycotting articles of common consumption from which the British Exchequer derives its chief revenue (a measure recommended long before by the Young Ireland Party), in favour of new systems of primary and secondary education, of competitive examinations for County Council appointments and of a National Banking System.

The Appeal which the National Council issued for support was based on the ground that the Council " denies the right of any foreign legislature to make laws to bind the people of Ireland, denies the authority of any foreign administration to exist in Ireland, and denies the wisdom of countenancing the existence of an usurped authority in Irish affairs by participating in the proceedings of the British Parliament."

## THE EARLY YEARS OF SINN FEIN

The two years following 1906 saw a great advance in the spread of Sinn Fein principles. Debates were organized with members of the other Nationalist organizations, reading rooms were established and lectures given. In Belfast, the Dungannon Club, a separatist organization which had for some time published a small and ably conducted paper called the *Republic*, as well as a series of pamphlets, now amalgamated with the West Belfast Branch of the National Council. Every care was taken to prevent the movement assuming a sectional as distinct from a national tendency. Every instance of intolerance towards a fellow-Irishman committed by members of any political party was faithfully pilloried in the columns of *Sinn Fein*. When the Westport Guardians (for example) demanded the dismissal of Canon Hannay from his chaplaincy for being the author of *The Seething Pot*, which offended the political sensibilities of the worthy Guardians, he found no more strenuous advocate, and the Guardians no more unsparing critic, than *Sinn Fein*. In Dublin the movement was particularly strong, and even succeeded in securing the return of some of its candidates at the elections to the City Council. When the Liberal Government in 1906 offered Mr. Redmond, in place of a Home Rule Bill, what was known as the Devolution Bill, the sincerity of English parties in their dealings with Ireland began to be widely questioned and Sinn Fein received an additional impetus. An official Sinn Fein handbook, "Leabhar na hEireann,

## 80 THE EVOLUTION OF SINN FEIN

the Irish Year Book," was published containing, in addition to articles on the Sinn Fein policy, a number of valuable statistics with reference to Irish resources, enterprises, movements and parties, both political and religious. At last in 1908 the time seemed to have come for contesting a parliamentary election. Mr. C. J. Dolan, the sitting member for North Leitrim, declared himself a convert to the new movement. He resigned his seat and offered himself for re-election as a Sinn Fein candidate. He polled less than a third of the votes, and Sinn Fein received a serious setback. In fact the ground had not been sufficiently prepared. A weekly paper, supplemented by a few pamphlets, with no great circulation outside Dublin, was an insufficient instrument with which to achieve the success of a new policy within two years. It was proposed and attempted to repair the error by the establishment of a daily edition of *Sinn Fein*. But the movement had made no progress among the more prosperous classes. The paper was in difficulties from the start and an attempt to make it more popular by increasing it from four pages to eight committed it beyond recall to failure. Meanwhile a Sinn Fein Co-operative Bank had been established, and, pushing ahead, the party issued a programme to which candidates for election to all elected bodies in Ireland were to be asked to subscribe. They were asked to pledge themselves to support the independence of Ireland, a system of protection for Irish industries, the establishment of an Irish

## THE EARLY YEARS OF SINN FEIN 81

Consular Service and an Irish Mercantile Marine, a general survey and development of the mineral resources of Ireland, an Irish National Bank, National Stock Exchange and National Civil Service, National Courts of Arbitration, a National System of Insurance, National Control of Transit and Fisheries, a reform of the educational system, the abolition of the poorhouses, the gradual introduction of the Irish language as the official language of public boards. In addition they were to agree to refuse to recognize the British Parliament, and to discourage the consumption of articles paying duty to the British Treasury and the enlistment of Irishmen in the British Army.

This ambitious programme met with little or no response, and with the collapse of the daily paper the apathy of the general public became more marked. On the mass of Unionist Ireland, especially in Ulster, Sinn Fein had practically no influence. The movement for the reform of the financial relations between England and Ireland which had followed the publication of the Report of the Financial Relations Committee in 1896 had been the last All-Ireland movement in which Unionist Ulster had taken part. But after a brief period of enthusiasm the movement had come to nothing. Though the Report showed that Ireland had been since the Union, and partly in contravention of the express terms of that Act, the victim of grave financial injustice, being over-taxed to the amount of two-and-three-quarter millions of

pounds per annum, nothing was done to remedy
the grievance. The English Government was
obdurate: the landlords gradually ceased to take
any prominent part in the movement for fear of
prejudicing their class interests. Unionist Ireland, especially in Ulster, allowed its morbid
suspicion of everything in which the rest of the
country was interested to overbear (as usual) its
patriotism and its common sense, and Nationalist
Ireland lost interest in the matter in pursuit of
other objects. The Financial Reform Association
had been dissolved in 1899 and the country settled
down again to the old political struggle. The
Nationalist Party fought shy of the raising of all
fundamental questions. Its policy was to "wrest
from whatever Government was in power the full
measure of a nation's rights," that is to say, to
gain as full a measure of Home Rule from either
Liberals or Conservatives as the exigencies of
English politics and the opinion of the English
public might make possible. Their aim was not
to educate Irish public opinion or to convince Irish
opposition. It was taken for granted that the
Liberal Party would some day bring in a Home
Rule Bill and carry it against the Conservative
Party, and that that would end the matter: that
the Conservatives (according to the English party
system of government) would accept "the verdict
of the people," yielding to the inevitable, and that
the Irish Unionists would have to follow suit. To
discuss the fundamentals of the problem, to endeavour to unite Irishmen (so far as argument and a

generally understood common interest could unite
them) was tiresome, irrelevant and tending to the
subversion of party discipline. For the policy
now adopted by the Parliamentarians " a united
party" was above all things essential; and the
unity desired meant not merely a common aim but
an agreement upon all details: the great offence
was " faction," and under faction was comprised
all independent criticism either of policy or of
principle. A party thus constituted was, if things
went well and it was wisely led, an invaluable
instrument of parliamentary warfare at Westminster; but if things went wrong or a mistake
was made, or if Westminster should cease at any
time to be the centre of interest, disaster was sure
to follow. And this conception of the duty of an
Irish National Party overlooked the possibilities
latent in Ulster Unionism. To an extent, not at
the time fully grasped by anyone in Ireland, it
stood not for the Unionist Party, as that party was
understood in England, but for itself alone. The
exigencies of party warfare required that it, like
the Nationalist Party, should attach itself to an
English party; that it should adopt the parlance
of English parties; that it should declare its un-
bending loyalty to Imperial interests and the
British Constitution. But it was not inclined to
admit in practice that the British Constitution
could override its own particular interests. It
could not be ignored or flouted with impunity;
it was the rock upon which all schemes based upon
the peaceful possibilities of English parliamentary

situations were destined in the end to make shipwreck.

But the rock was not yet in sight and its existence was unsuspected. It was common ground to the two Irish parties that the arena was Parliament and that the prize should go to the party which won the game according to Westminster rules. It is easy now for those who kept their eyes shut to say that they would have opened them if everybody else had not been born blind, and it would be more dignified to say nothing. But the fact remains that the mistake was made.

During the lean years for its policy that followed 1908, *Sinn Fein* continued persistently to preach its doctrines: that to obtain " the full measure of a nation's rights" Ireland must rely not upon outside aid but upon her own efforts: that all Irishmen had a common interest, and that interest not the interest of England: that all Irishmen, whether called Nationalist or Unionist, were brothers in a common country impoverished and weakened by the loss of independence resulting from the Act of Union, and that to recognize their common interests and understand one another was their immediate object. It published articles on the destruction of Irish industries in the interests of those of England, a destruction arrested by the Constitution of 1782, and acting without restraint since the loss of that Constitution by the Act of Union. It welcomed literary contributions by the most eminent Irish men of letters, without distinction of politics or religion: it preached un-

## THE EARLY YEARS OF SINN FEIN 85

ceasingly the doctrines of toleration and goodwill amongst Irishmen. But as the prospect of the triumph of parliamentarianism through its alliance with the Liberal Party grew brighter, interest centred more and more upon the doings of Parliament and the vicissitudes of parliamentary fortunes. Now at last the dream of a century was to take shape in something resembling a substance, and the time for discussion, arrangement and accommodation was over. In April, 1910, *Sinn Fein* announced on behalf of its party that Mr. John Redmond, having now the chance of a lifetime to obtain Home Rule, will be given a free hand, without a word said to embarrass him. But it was difficult not to speak sometimes. When the Liberal Budget left the House of Commons that month, before the veto of the House of Lords had been abolished, Mr. Redmond's acquiescence in these tactics was freely censured. When in the autumn of the same year Mr. Redmond committed himself to the declaration: " We do not want' to discontinue our representation in the House of Commons when Home Rule comes; we desire to have Irish members sitting at Westminster not only to form a nucleus of the ultimate Federal Parliament of the Empire, but also to assist in legislation concerning Great Britain and Ireland collectively," the declaration was quoted with disgust. The Home Rule of the Liberal Party was indeed far removed from the Constitution of 1782.

Sinn Fein took no official part in the elections of 1910, preferring, as it said in its official organ, to remain "wholly free from any moral responsibility" for the legislation offered by the Liberals to the Parliamentary Party, while retaining the right to examine, criticise and warn. This was not purely an act of self-sacrifice. In fact Sinn Fein was never at so low an ebb. While the country was drifting farther and farther in the direction of Home Rule, Sinn Fein was insisting more and more upon first principles. Its official attitude of warm approval of the work of the Gaelic League was exchanged for one of insistence upon the urgency of making Irish the national language. "We must begin again," said *Sinn Fein*, " to be an Irish-speaking people, or there can be no future of national independence before us." With England on the one hand and America on the other, 120,000,000 people speaking English, the danger to the language was imminent. "We freely admit," it proceeded, "that this conclusion is not one we sought nor one we desired. The conviction has forced itself upon us and has been with some reluctance accepted by us." And it continued to speak plain language about the Home Rule which now seemed inevitable: "No scheme which the English Parliament may pass in the near future will satisfy Sinn Fein—no legislature created in Ireland which is not supreme and absolute will offer a basis for concluding a final settlement with the foreigners who usurp the government of this country. But any measure which gives genuine, if even partial, control of their own affairs to Irishmen shall meet with no opposition from us

## THE EARLY YEARS OF SINN FEIN 87

and should meet with no opposition from any section of Irishmen." So far was Sinn Fein at this time from any desire to do more than infuse a new spirit into Irishmen, favourable to the eventual future development of the policy outlined by the National Council, that it expressly disclaimed the title of a party. " It is not our business," was the conclusion of a pamphlet issued by the Belfast Branch of Sinn Fein, " to make one more party among the political parties of Ireland, nor to carry on a party propaganda nor to waste time quarrelling with any political party. Above the cries of contending parties we raise the cry of Ireland and Irish independence—an independence in the gaining of which Catholic and Protestant will be shoulder comrades as they were a century ago, and in the advantages of which they will be equal sharers. Not an Ireland for a class or a creed, but an Ireland for the Irish, and the whole of the Irish, not an Ireland fettered and trammelled by England, but mistress of her own destinies, evolving her own national life and building for herself an ever-increasing prosperity. We can leave the past with its bitter memories, its bigotries and its feuds to those whose property it is, the reactionaries who here, as in every country, would stem the tide of national advancement. We have to recognise the nation, rather than parties within the nation; for it is greater than any party, and in the service of the nation all men have an equal right as well as an equal duty."

## SINN FEIN AND THE REPUBLICANS.

From 1910 to 1913 the Sinn Fein movement was practically moribund. Political attention in Ireland was largely centred on the fate of Home Rule and the tactics of the Irish Party at Westminster or the struggles of the Party at home with Mr. William O'Brien and the All-for-Ireland League. The Constitution which Ireland might enjoy in 1914 was of more pressing interest than the merits of the Constitution of 1782.

But there were other forces at work in Ireland in opposition to the two official parties of Unionists and Nationalists. There were in the first place the survivors of the Fenians, the Irish Republican Brotherhood, whose ideal was an Irish Republic, independent of any connection with England or indeed with any other country. Fenianism had become to all outward appearance practically dead in Ireland. It had suffered, in the opinion of some at least of its members, from the fact that it had put revolutionary action first and the preaching of republicanism second. As one of them wrote afterwards, " The Fenian propagandist work in the sixties was entirely separatist with practically no reference to Republicanism. Rightly or wrongly I have always held the view that the absence of the deeper Republican thought amongst our people accounted for a considerable amount of the falling away after '67." The people whose republican sentiments were weak " dropped back into the easier path leading only to a much modified national independence." Accordingly after 1867 the Fenians attempted to make republicanism an essential part of their propaganda. There had been a large number of Protestant Irishmen among the Fenians, and, as Republican sentiment had been traditional in Ulster since the days of the United Irishmen, it seemed that a movement aiming at an Irish Republic might have more chance of success among Ulster Protestants than any form of " Home Rule." Besides, the " New Departure," the alliance of Fenianism with Parnell in the Land War, had weakened the movement still more. " It was disastrous," says the same authority, "to the Fenian movement as such, but it drove the Land League through to a degree that no really constitutional movement could ever have reached." In allying itself to some extent with Parnell, in abandoning for the time in his interests its revolutionary propaganda, it seemed to have weakened its own moral force, while it did not succeed in winning even Home Rule. And the fact of its being of necessity a secret society brought it under the ban of the Church. Fear of ecclesiastical censure most often kept young Irishmen out of Fenianism. It was not enough for the Fenians to say, as they did, that to the existence of a secret society whose aims were lawful there was no moral or theological objection. The experts in morals and theology said that there was, and their word, and not that of the Fenians, was accepted on the whole as final. And the actions of the Invincibles during the Parnellite struggle had gravely compromised not Parnell only but the Fenian Party, to which they were supposed to belong. As a matter of fact the Irish Republican Brotherhood had nothing to do with them. It had no sympathy with, nor reliance on, their policy of political assassination. A member of the Brotherhood who joined the Invincibles was regarded as having broken his oath to its members and its constitution. But this was not generally believed, any more than Parnell's statement that he had been no party to the brutal murder of Lord Frederick Cavendish; and the prestige of Fenianism was lowered. Still, the Irish Republican Brotherhood was in existence as a centre of separatist and republican thought and the imminence of Home Rule could not but stimulate its interest. Its members must either decide to lend their support to Mr. Redmond as it had once been lent to Parnell, or to come out, whether openly or in private, as his opponents.

The Irish Republican Brotherhood was not the only centre of republican thought in Ireland. In 1896 the Irish Socialist Republican Party had been founded in Dublin by James Connolly, the ablest organizer and writer which Irish Labour has yet produced. Under his editorship *The Workers' Republic* became an organ of Socialism and Republicanism in their application to Irish conditions. The new party took its part in Irish political activities. It joined the movement to commemorate the Rebellion of 1798, the work of the United Irishmen whose political creed had been republican. Along with other Irish Nationalists it joined in the work of the Irish Transvaal Committee and helped to organize and equip the Irish Brigade which fought on the side of the South African Republics. But till after the General Election of 1910 it made no attempt to enter Irish politics as an independent party. It remained in its constitution a purely trade union party though sympathetic with, and ready to lend its aid in, the Irish national movement. In 1911 the proposal to found a combined political and industrial movement was defeated by only three votes at the Congress held at Galway, and in the following year the Clonmel Congress decided to found " an Irish Labour Party independent of all other parties in the country, in order that the organized workers might be able to enter the proposed Irish Parliament as an organized Labour Party upon the political field." Though the Irish Labour Party was not professedly republican, and though its political activities were confined for the time to the enforcement of the political interests of Irish Labour, yet the leaders and a considerable number of the rank and file were undoubtedly republican in their aims and sympathies.

The Irish Labour Party had need, in truth, to be independent of all existing political parties in Ireland. The Ulster Unionist Party was definitely and irrevocably committed to the Conservative and

capitalist programme. It would as soon have
admitted to its ranks a professed dynamitard as
a professed socialist (whatever his views might
have been on the subject of the Legislative Union).
On Socialism the Church could not be expected
to smile (and did not smile) and its attitude determined
that of the Irish Parliamentary Party.
The Party was in a delicate position: it could not
say a word against Socialism for fear of offending
the English Labour Party, whose votes were
required in the parliamentary struggle: it could
not say a word in favour of it for fear of offending
the Church. It was sitting upon a razor's edge
and a word too much in either direction might
easily disturb its balance. So it voted steadily,
manfully and silently for Labour measures in
England and left its action to the country. In
the frame-work of the Sinn Fein programme there
was no place for Labour. Among all its plans for
the relief of Ireland from the evils of the English
connection there was none for the relief of the
evils of which the workers complained. Its
official organ was against strikes, and even considered
that the connection of Irish with English
Labour was an act of treachery to the country.
Some of the most pungent criticism to which the
party was subjected came from the paper founded
in 1911 by James Larkin, *The Irish Worker and
People's Advocate*. In its first number, the editor
defined his attitude to the O'Brienites, the Irish
Parliamentary Party and Sinn Fein. He described
the last as a "party or rump which, while pre-

tending to be Irish of the Irish, insults the nation by trying to foist on it not only imported economics based on false principles, but which had the temerity to advocate the introduction of foreign capitalists into this sorely exploited country." "Their chief appeal" (he goes on) " to the foreign capitalists was that they (the imported capitalists) would have freedom to employ cheap Irish labour . . . . For eleven years these self-appointed prophets and seers have led their army up the hill and led them down again, and would continue to so lead them, if allowed, until the leader was appointed King of Ireland under the Constitution of 1782."

The definitely Republican movement found an organ of expression in the autumn of 1910 by the establishment of *Saoirseacht na h-Eireann, Irish Freedom*, a fortnightly paper of eight pages, under the management of Seaghan MacDiarmada. Its motto was a quotation from Wolfe Tone: " To subvert the tyranny of our execrable Government, to break the connection with England, the never-failing source of all our political evils and to assert the independence of my country—these were my objects." Its policy was explained at length in its editorial: " We believe that free political institutions are an absolute essential for the future security and development of the Irish people and, therefore, we seek to establish free political institutions in this country; and in this we wish not to be the organ of any party, but the organ of an uncompromising Nationalism. We stand not for an Irish party but for National tradition—the tradition of Wolfe Tone and Robert Emmet, of John Mitchel and John O'Leary. Like them we believe in and would work for the independence of Ireland—and we use the term with no reservation stated or implied; we stand for the complete and total separation of Ireland from England and the establishment of an Irish Government, untrammelled and uncontrolled by any other Government in the world. Like them we stand for an Irish Republic—for, as Thomas Devin Reilly said in 1848, 'Freedom can take but one shape amongst us—a Republic.'"

The attitude of this new republican movement to that of the previous Sinn Fein movement is clearly defined in a subsequent leader. "The temporary suspension of the Sinn Fein movement is often cited as a throwback but it is nothing of the kind. Under whatever name we propagate our ideas the Irish Nation must be built on Sinn Fein principles, or non-recognition of British authority, law, justice or legislature: that is our basis and the principles of the Sinn Fein policy are as sound to-day as ever they were. The movement is temporarily suspended because some of its leaders directed it into an '82 movement, thinking they could collar the middle-classes and drop the separatists; but when the separatists were dropped there was no movement left."

The new movement was in fact an attempt to rehabilitate and re-establish the Sinn Fein movement by making it definitely republican while adhering to the main lines of the policy by which Sinn Fein hoped to succeed. But the original Sinn Fein continued on its way. Its paper continued to be published and to find readers. It was unrepentant with regard to its political aims: "We do not care a fig for republicanism as republicanism," said *Sinn Fein* two years later; but from the winter of 1910 dates the movement which eventually drove out of Sinn Fein the idea of the re-establishment of the King, Lords and Commons of Ireland under the Constitution of 1782 and replaced it by that of an Irish Republic.

The new movement was the direct outcome of the Wolfe Tone Clubs. It was they who carried out all the work entailed by the publication of *Irish Freedom*. These clubs had just been founded " to propagate the principles and disseminate the teachings of Theobald Wolfe Tone and the other true Irishmen who in 1798, 1803, 1848 and 1867 strove for the complete independence of Ireland; to encourage the union of Irishmen of all creeds and sections in working for the freedom of their country; to promote the advancement of national thought and inculcate the spirit of self-sacrifice and self-reliance by which alone true liberty can be attained." The members pledged themselves to substitute the common name of Irishman for that of Catholic or Protestant; no person serving in the armed forces of England was eligible for membership.

This new branch of the Sinn Fein movement attempted to do what the old Sinn

Fein had not as yet done, get into direct
touch with labour questions and the labour
movement, though perhaps not very successfully.
The first number of *Irish Freedom* had an article
on sweated industries, pointing out that though
Nationalists talked as if Belfast were the only
place in Ireland where workers were underpaid,
many Nationalists were open to the same reproach.
It pointed out the duty of the universities in the
matter, pleading for a really scientific study of
Irish economic problems, including (besides the
wages system) such questions as the working of
the Land Acts, Co-operation, the conditions of the
Congested Districts. It welcomed with enthusiasm
the Co-operative Movement. "The co-operative
spirit," it said, "is perhaps the greatest asset in
modern Ireland and it will require a stronger flame
than the speeches of political firebrands to melt it
away." On the occasion of the strikes in Belfast,
Dublin, Cork and other towns in 1911 it took sides
with the strikers, in marked contrast to Mr.
Griffith's *Sinn Fein*, which preached something
approaching "abject surrender" on the part of
the workers. It induced Mr. George Russell to
contribute an article on the Co-operative Commonwealth. This undoubtedly went a certain way to
bring about a friendlier feeling on the part of
Labour towards Sinn Fein, but it was long before
the attitude of strict Sinn Feiners was forgotten
by the workers. Its attitude towards Ulster was
more outspoken and definite. In 1910 the objection of Ulster to the approaching Home Rule

policy of the Liberals began to harden into a threat of extreme militancy. A section of Ulster Unionists announced their intention not to submit under any circumstances to the Home Rule Bill even if it should become law and receive the Royal assent. To the Republicans this seemed " tantamount to an admission of the whole Irish case for self-government. If it means anything it means that Ireland, north as well as south of the Boyne, refuses to recognize any inherent right of the electors of Great Britain to decide how it shall be governed." The justness of this appreciation of the Ulster position must be examined later: but, true or false, it is characteristic of the attitude which the whole Sinn Fein Party was afterwards to take. But the Ulstermen coupled with their attitude towards the Liberal Party and its doings a truculent defiance of all Catholic Ireland. The cause of this hostility the Republicans found in the attitude of the Parliamentary Party. While that party was in the height of its success " no attempt was made to understand their [*i.e.* the Ulster Protestants'] attitude or grapple with problems that appealed to them, and the economic grievances of Belfast workers were regarded as their own affair, not as the business of men who professed to represent the Irish people as a whole. The prevailing idea seemed to be that they should be left to stew in their own juice, and if they did not fall in with whatever scheme the Liberals carried through the English Parliament that they should be, in the phrase of a prominent parliamentarian, which has never been forgotten, 'overborne by the strong hand.' .... The party of the future must make the conversion of Ulster the first plank in their platform and recognize that a national settlement from which Ulster dissented would not be worth winning." In the Ancient Order of Hibernians, all sections of Sinn Fein as well as the Labour Party saw a menace to any prospect of an accommodation with Ulster. This strictly sectarian society, as sectarian and often as violent in its methods as the Orange Lodges, evoked their determined hostility. "This narrowing down," wrote *Irish Freedom*, "of Nationalism to the members of one creed is the most fatal thing that has taken place in Irish politics since the days of the Pope's Brass Band. .... That the driving power of the official Nationalists should be supplied by an organization of which no Protestant, however good a patriot, can be a member, is in direct opposition to the policy and traditions of Irish Nationalism." The Ancient Order was described as "a job-getting and job-cornering organization," as "a silent practical rivetting of sectarianism on the nation." The *Irish Worker* was equally emphatic. "Were it not for the existence of the Board of Erin, the Orange Society would have long since ceased to exist. . . . To Brother Devlin and not to Brother Carson is mainly due the progress of the Covenanter movement in Ulster."

Devoted to the cause of an independent Irish Republic and of the union of Irishmen without distinction of creed under one national banner, the cause of Wolfe Tone, the movement attracted idealists who had so far held aloof from the older, non-republican, form of Sinn Fein. Chief among these were P. H. Pearse and Thomas MacDonagh, both poets and men of fine literary gifts, both regarded with affection for their high and disinterested devotion to the cause of Ireland. And in accordance with Irish Republican tradition it took up an attitude with regard to armed revolution somewhat different from that of Sinn Fein. While the latter held that in the present state of Ireland an armed revolution was impracticable, the Republicans, though not directly advising it, held that it had a reasonable prospect of success if England should become involved in a European War. Some Irish revolutionists who had so far held aloof from all political parties were encouraged by this to join the republican branch of Sinn Fein and try to infuse into it a more determined revolutionary spirit.

The Labour Party, whose opinions were expressed by the *The Irish Worker and People's Advocate*, adopted a similar attitude. Their motto was the phrase of Fintan Lalor: " The principle I state and mean to stand upon is this—that the entire ownership of Ireland, moral and material, up to the sun and down to the centre, is vested in the people of Ireland." Their own language was equally explicit: " By Freedom we mean that we Irishmen in Ireland shall be free to govern this land called Ireland by Irish people in the interest of all the Irish people; that no other people or peoples, no matter what they call themselves, or from whence they come, now or in the future, have any claim to interfere with the common right of the common people of this land of Ireland to work out their own destiny. We owe no allegiance to any other nation, nor the king, governors or representatives of any other nation." In spite of the criticism that a purely Labour movement should confine itself to Labour questions, and leave the broader political issues to the one side, *The Irish Worker* declared for an independent Irish Republic: " We know," it said, " that until the workers of Ireland obtain possession of the land of Ireland and make their own laws they can only hope for and obtain partial improvement of their conditions. We ask no more than our rights: we will be content with no less." The desire for a " free independent nation, enjoying a true Republican freedom " linked the Labour Party to the republican branch of Sinn Fein, but on other questions there was much disagreement. The attitude of Arthur Griffith to the Wexford Strike in 1911 was the subject of bitter comment. The Young Republicans, who objected to English Trade Unions sending " English money " to finance the Irish strikers, were bluntly told to mind their own business: the Gaelic League, which encouraged Irish manufactures, was said to have failed in its duty by taking no account of the conditions under which they were manufactured, or of the wages paid to the workers who made them: " the revival of the Irish language is a desirable ambition and has our whole-hearted support; but the abolition of destitution, disease and the conditions that cause them are even more necessary and urgent. What is the use of bilingualism to a dead man?"

But however they might differ on minor points, both of these new parties, the Independent Labour Party of Ireland and the Young Republican Party, were at one with each other and with Sinn Fein in opposition to the Parliamentary Party. It was pointed out that in the twenty-one years which had elapsed since the death of Parnell his policy of " blocking the way to English legislation until Ireland was accorded self-government " had been abandoned without any other definite policy being substituted for it: that during ten of those years an English party, professing sympathy with Ireland, had been kept in office by the Irish vote: that Home Rule was still in the future and the principles governing the expected measure still undetermined. In March, 1912, the Executive of Sinn Fein resolved unanimously: " That this Executive earnestly hopes that the promised Home Rule Bill will be one that may be accepted as a genuine measure of reform by the people of Ireland and that it may speedily become law. Should the Bill, on the contrary, be rejected as unsatisfactory by the people of Ireland, or should it, though satisfactory, fail to become law—which we would deplore—the organization is prepared to lead the country by other and effective methods to the attainment of self-government." In reporting this resolution *Sinn Fein* wrote, in words which at the time seemed to many supporters of the Party offensive, but which now seem charged with portent: " No new parliamentarian movement will be permitted unopposed to build upon the ruins of that which goes down with a sham Home Rule measure. To make this clear before the Home Rule measure be introduced is the last service we can render the Parliamentary Party. They have had the Government ' in the hollow of their hands' for years—they have removed the House of Lords from their path—there is nothing to prevent the Liberal Government introducing and passing a full measure of Home Rule save and except its enmity to Ireland. With a majority of over 100 and the Lords' veto removed the fullest measure of Home Rule can be passed in two years. It is the business of the Parliamentary Party to have it passed or to leave the stage to those who are in earnest."

The appearance of the text of the Bill was not reassuring even to those advocates of Irish independence who were willing to take a measure of Home Rule as an instalment. The financial provisions of the Bill met with severe and justified criticism. In spite of the fact that Ireland had been systematically over-taxed for a century, and that a Parliamentary Commission had so reported nearly twenty years earlier, the financial provision for the proposed Irish Parliament could only be described as beggarly. And almost everything that really mattered in the government of Ireland was withdrawn from the competence of the Irish Parliament. It was described in mockery as a "Gas and Water Bill," and even convinced supporters of the Parliamentary Party had their qualms in declaring their acceptance of the measure. There was no dubiety about the verdict of the Nationalist organizations opposed to Mr. Redmond. *The Worker's Republic* was outspoken in the extreme: it complained that the Bill had been extorted from the Liberals " by whining and apologizing": in an Open Letter to the United Irish League of Great Britain, it said, " You are told that the people of Ireland accepted the Bill as a full and complete recognition of our claim as Irishmen. That is a lie . . . . a Bill, which is the rottenest bargain ever made by a victorious people with a mean, pettifogging, despised Government." " A beggar," it wrote again, " gets only crumbs and we, Irish workers, want a country." The verdict of *Irish Freedom* was equally emphatic; it was summed up in the phrase, " Damn your concessions; we want our country."

But whatever individual Irish Members of Parliament may have thought of the Bill, the Party was as a whole committed to it. No one in Ireland knew what negotiations, barterings, and bargains preceded the actual drafting of the measure: what the difficulties and objections were which had to be met by Mr. Redmond: in how far he had offered concessions, in how far they had been forced upon him. They only knew that he was prepared to support the resulting Bill and that the resulting Bill was less than they had been led to expect. There was little open discussion of principles, criticism was not relished or welcomed. The Party had done its best for the country and the country was now called upon to back the Party. A bargain had been made by the representatives of the Irish people and the Irish people were expected to stand by the consequences. Under other circumstances this appeal would have been accepted, but it was no answer to the complaint that the Irish representatives had not been empowered to abandon in express words every national claim that went beyond those satisfied by the provisions of the Home Rule Bill. This was the kernel of the dispute between the Party and the Nationalists who opposed them. It seemed as if by the deliberate renunciation of any desire or intention to claim for Ireland anything more than the status of a dependency of Great Britain, deprived forever (so far as an act of legislation could deprive her) of her immemorial claim to be an independent nation, the Party had betrayed the national demand and sold the national honour. But the Party did not see (or betrayed no sign of having seen) the relevance of the criticism; and certainly they miscalculated the strength of the opposition which was gathering in the country. In the face of Ulster's attitude, they confidently expected the whole country to rally to their support. And, after all, what could, or would, the dissentients do about it? Sinn Fein continued loudly to proclaim its policy of opposition to the use of force. It was all very well to say " Sinn Fein is the policy of to-morrow. If Ireland be again deceived as to Home Rule, she has no other policy to fall back upon"; but the same article (December, 1912) contained the words: " The great offence of Sinn Fein indeed in the eyes of its opponents is that it does not urge an untrained and unequipped country to futile insurrection." If Sinn Fein then would only talk, and the only place to talk to the purpose was the House of Commons, what was there to prevent Home Rule from being an accomplished fact " in the not far distant future?" Ulster supplied the answer, not for itself only, but for the rest of Ireland.

## THE VOLUNTEER MOVEMENT.

The genius of Ulster (perhaps through some happy combination of primitive stocks) has always been practical and militant. It was the last Irish province to submit to English rule. The Celtic population which survived the clearances and the plantings has exercised upon planters and settlers the ancient charm of the Celtic stock and made them, in spite of themselves, *ipsis Hibernis Hiberniores*. The O'Neills were the most formidable antagonists whom the invaders encountered in Ireland. They made the last great stand for national independence. When Owen Roe O'Neill died the Irish nation was, in the words of Davis, " sheep without a shepherd when the snow shuts out the sky" and the flight of the Earls was the sign that the resistance of Ireland was over with the resistance of Ulster. In later times and under changed conditions Ulster retained the prerogative of leadership. The Volunteers who forced the Constitution of 1782 were largely Ulstermen; the leaders of the United Irishmen were to be found in Ulster and the compact of their Union was sealed on the mountain that rises above Belfast. John Mitchel, who led the Young Irelanders in action as Davis was their master in

## THE VOLUNTEER MOVEMENT 107

thought, was the son of an Ulster Presbyterian minister. Other Irishmen may have excelled in literature and the arts, have voiced more eloquently the aspirations of their country or sung with more pathos of its fall, but the bent of Ulster has been on the whole towards action and movement. The heart and brain of Ireland may beat and think elsewhere, but Ulster is its right arm. Ireland is proud of Ulster. Under an unnatural and vicious system of government they have quarrelled; but if Ulster were reconciled to Ireland Ulster might lead it where it chose.

On the question of the Home Rule Bill Ulster was almost equally divided. The majority of the Ulster Protestants were against it, though a minority, among whom traditions of Protestant Nationalism had survived the sordid bigotries fostered for a century, were strongly in its favour; the majority of the Catholic population were in favour of it. Among the Nationalists there was a minority who professed the creed of Sinn Fein and of Republicanism: late in 1913 a branch of the Young Republican Party in Belfast, composed of Gaelic Leaguers, members of Freedom Clubs and Trades Unionists unfurled its banner of an orange sunburst on a green ground with the motto in white, "Young Republican Party—Dia agus an Pobul," and there had been branches of Sinn Fein established in Ulster some years earlier; but on the whole the Ulster Nationalists supported the Parliamentary Party. No geographical or ethnological line of political demarcation could be drawn.

There was no district in Ulster which was not politically divided: there was no stock in Ulster which had not members in both political camps. Some of the most outspoken and vehement of the Unionist Party bore, and were proud of, purely Irish names; many of the Nationalists were the bearers of names introduced into Ireland with the planters sent by King James. The settled policy of the Act of the Union had done its work with almost complete success. The Protestant had learned to regard the connection with England as essential to the maintenance of his religious and civil freedom: he believed not only that the Roman Catholic Church was officially intolerant, but that all Roman Catholics were, as a matter of fact, intolerant in conduct and in practice, and incapable of being anything else. And Irish Catholics seemed to him to be peculiarly susceptible to the intolerant influences of their ecclesiastical leaders. When the views of the Catholic Hierarchy in Ireland and those of Irish Nationalists coincided he saw in their agreement the triumph of the " priest in politics ": when they differed he was either at a loss to account for an occurrence so far removed from the settled habits of nature or saw in it an obscure but interesting symptom of a fear of Home Rule on the part of the Hierarchy, a fear that Home Rule might jeopardise their own predominance. But not even the supposed hesitations of the Hierarchy could reconcile him to the prospect of a Home Rule under which the electoral majority

## THE VOLUNTEER MOVEMENT 109

would be " priest-ridden." Unkind critics might have urged that people whose whole political outlook was hag-ridden by the phantoms of popes and priests were not in a position to call those " priest-ridden" who at any rate sometimes differed sharply from their clergy in political and civil affairs; but the Ulster Protestant was proof against mere logical quibbles and rhetorical retorts. He had done his thinking about politics with the Act of Union: he had taken his stand: he was careless of taunts, cajolery and threats: let those meddle with him who dared. He spurned the allegation of intolerance, but he was intolerant without knowing it and (to do him justice) for reasons which, had they corresponded with the facts, would have been sound. An Ireland under ecclesiastical despotism, whether Protestant cr Catholic, would be no place for a man to live in, and to exchange the Legislative Union with England for a legislative union with Rome would indeed be a disastrous bargain. As a matter of fact, had the Ulster Protestant realized it, there was no fear of any such result. In the Irish Catholic mind there was clearly defined the limit of the sphere in which the Church was supreme. That sphere was much larger than the restricted area within which the Protestant allowed his Church to legislate at its ease: but it was subject to limitations all the same. And it was growing narrower and narrower. Individual ecclesiastics may have roamed at large (and did roam at large) over the whole sphere of human activities: individual priests made monstrous claims upon the submission of their flocks in matters with which they had no kind of concern. The intense devotion to their religion which marks Catholic Irishmen, the respect which they feel for the priesthood which stood by them in dark and evil days, had induced a spirit of patience in submission to claims which could not be substantiated. But with the revival of interest in political thought the position was changing. The battle for political freedom of thought and action which the Fenians had fought had its result. Ecclesiastical claims in civil matters were subject to a close scrutiny. The Gaelic League had more than once asserted with success its claim to be free in its own sphere from any kind of ecclesiastical dictation, and in every instance the people of Ireland has taken its side. The attempt of the Roman Curia to interfere with the subscription to the Parnell testimonial had been an ignominious failure; and the boast of an Irish leader that he would as soon take his politics from Constantinople as from Rome was generally acknowledged to be sound as a statement of theory. But there were still instances enough of impossible claims on the part of the ecclesiastical authorities to afford the Ulster Protestant a good *prima facie* brief against Home Rule.

Allied to the fear of the " priest in politics " was the fear that under Home Rule every position in Ireland worth speaking of would be given to Roman Catholics and that Protestants would be systematically and, ruthlessly excluded. This was an apprehension very difficult to deal with because the real grounds of it were seldom openly expressed. These grounds were first, the consciousness that Irish Catholics had been for generations systematically excluded from all posts that were in the gift of Irish Protestants and the consequent probability that reprisals would be called for and taken; second, the innate conviction, born of generations of religious controversy and suspicion, that Catholics were " not to be trusted," that, whatever they said to the contrary, they were certain to act harshly towards Protestants, and that the accession to power in Ireland of a permanent Catholic majority would mean persecution in matters of religion and corruption in matters of administration. This position was fortified by a set of arguments, crude in themselves, but less crude than the convictions that required to employ them. It was pointed out that Irish Catholics, being deprived for generations of acceptable opportunities of higher education, and of practically all opportunities of administrative experience, could not be expected to have the necessary qualifications for the posts to which they were certain to be appointed: that this was not their fault (it certainly was not) but that, facts being facts, reasonable persons must take account of them and frame their attitude in accordance with them. It may seem strange that all this was called " adherence to the principles of civil and religious liberty," that persons calling for religious toleration in the abstract should refuse to practise it in

any number of given cases: but though there was
a certain amount of conscious artifice in the use of
words, arising from a dim feeling that the
profession of tolerant and liberal sentiments was
more likely to arouse outside sympathy than a
blunt statement of religious prejudice, there was,
after all, the idea that the only way to preserve
civil and religious liberty in Ireland for anybody
was to curtail its exercise in practice by the Roman
Catholic and Nationalist portion of the country.
It was easy for Catholics to point to the number
of Protestants who had been honoured and trusted
leaders of the national movement, to the friendly
terms upon which Protestants and Catholics for the
most part lived together in the South and West of
Ireland, to the Protestants who had been appointed
to positions of trust and profit under boards and
in institutions managed by Irish Catholics. The
answer was that such Protestants either were the
only persons who could be trusted to perform the
duties of their position or had proved "accommodating" enough to suit, or that their appointment
was part of a deep-laid plan to conceal the real
feeling of Catholics to Protestants until such time
as, the bait being taken, Protestants would confide
in their enemies and hand themselves over to their
mercies.

It is evident that no line of argument would have
dispelled feelings such as these; and there does not
seem to be in fact any possibility of dispelling
them by mere professions of friendliness, or by
any other means than an experience to the contrary

## THE VOLUNTEER MOVEMENT 113

which can build up gradually an opposite conviction.

The religious difficulty was the root difficulty in Ulster with regard to Home Rule. If it had been removed or removable the rest would have been easy; but it was not the only difficulty. There was the fear, widely held by the Belfast merchants and manufacturers, that a Home Rule Parliament would ruin their industries: directly by means of taxation and indirectly by public mismanagement. It was held that an Irish Parliament could not " pay its way " without the imposition of extra taxation, and that no source of profitable taxation was to be found in Ireland save and except the prosperous industries of the North. In the second place, it was believed that, Ireland being largely agricultural, the new Parliament would represent a predominantly agricultural interest and that its legislation might be expected to fail to take into account the industrial interests of the country, mainly represented in the North. Again, an untried Parliament would for a time be almost certainly guilty of mismanagement and incapacity from which the business interests of the North would be sure to suffer.

Lastly, the strong " British " sentiment of Ulster barred the way to any weakening of the tie uniting Ireland to Great Britain. This feeling, amounting at times almost to the consciousness of a secondary nationality, found expression in the theory that Protestant Ulster was a separate " nation." But though the expression of the theory was often absurd, the feeling which underlay it was genuine. It had not been always there: it was liable to disappear under the stress of stronger feelings: it had been subject to revulsions. When the Irish Church Act was passed, the Grand Orange Lodge of Ireland, the Cardinalate of Ulster Protestantism, had passed by a majority the following resolution: "That all statements and provisions in the objects, rules and formularies of the Orange institution which impose any obligation on its members to maintain the Legislative Union between Great Britain and Ireland be expunged therefrom." The resolution was inoperative because a two-thirds majority was required to alter the rules: but that it could be passed is significant of the fact that "British" sentiment is not the ruling sentiment in the stronghold of Ulster Unionism under provocation. Still, though spasmodic and uncertain, the feeling had to be taken into account, and in the hands of skilful manipulators was capable of being worked into a factitious fervour.

While Ulster Unionists were of this mind it was not to be expected that they would acquiesce without protest in the passing of a Home Rule Act: nor was it to be expected that they would think differently because a majority of the electors of Great Britain decided that they should. The only people who could win them were their own countrymen. Sinn Fein saw this clearly and in its own way tried its best to allay Protestant fears and Protestant prejudices. *Irish Freedom* printed a letter from New York from an old Fenian who said, " The great barrier to Irish success is the fear of the Protestants—unfounded and unreasonable, but undeniably there—that their interests would be in danger in a free Ireland. Remove that fear and the Irish question is solved. It would be of infinitely more service to Ireland to convert ten Ulster Orangemen to Nationality by convincing them that their interests would be safe in a free Ireland than to convince a million Englishmen that the Irish would be loyal to the king. . . . We had many ex-Orangemen in Fenianism. . . . . All experience shows that it is easier to convert an Orangeman to full nationality than to any form of Home Rule." But for Irish Catholics to convert Irish Orangemen to anything requires infinite tact, infinite patience, and a long lapse of time: and it cannot be said that either the Sinn Fein or the Republican Party properly estimated the difficulty and complexity of the problem. The attempt to moderate the Ulster resistance by appeals to the principles of democratic government was, if possible, even less successful. It proved vain to urge that under democratic rule the will of the majority must prevail: that every party must expect to be in its turn in a minority and must learn to take the rough with the smooth: that the very principle and object of the Act of Union was that people in Ireland should not have the final say in the Government of Ireland but that the Parliament of the

United Kingdom should decide: that both parties in Ireland had acknowledged this principle for generations and that for the Nationalists to act as the Unionists were doing now would have been denounced by the Unionists themselves as an offence against good government. Appeal was made to Ulster in the interests of the Empire to allow Home Rule to have at least a fair trial. It was told that Englishmen were convinced that the government of Ireland was radically vicious, and that the only way to amend it was to entrust the internal affairs of Ireland to a strictly subordinate Parliament: that they felt that to continue in Ireland indefinitely an indefensible system of administration was to embitter the internal relations of the three kingdoms and weaken the Empire at the very centre. It was pointed out that a friendly Ireland would be worth many divisions of the Fleet and Army in the European struggle which could be seen to be approaching and the Ulster Unionists were asked to 'sacrifice' to the Empire what Parliament felt they ought no longer to retain.

Neither argument nor appeal had the least effect: the argument meant nothing to them and the appeal was supposed to imply that the argument was known to be unsound. They took their stand upon the Act of Union and declared that, it having once been passed, no Parliament had any right whatever to deprive the Unionists of Ulster of "their rights as British citizens." It was, of course, perfectly clear that, Home Rule or no

## THE VOLUNTEER MOVEMENT 117

Home Rule, everybody in the country was as much a British citizen as ever: and the idea that Parliament could not, if it pleased, repeal the Act of Union (which, as a matter of fact, it was very far indeed from proposing to do) was quite absurd. The fact is that all parties were at cross purposes and that a great many politicians were using language which meant one thing to themselves and another thing to everybody else, while a certain number were using language which they were perfectly well aware did not express what they really meant. " Loyalty to the Empire" did not mean the same thing to the Prime Minister and to the Orange orators who held the ear of Ulster; and when the latter professed sentiments of toleration and good will to " their Catholic fellow-countrymen" (as they sometimes did) they must have known that they were using words which they did not mean literally and strictly. At the bottom of everything was the conviction that, Protestantism being a superior kind of religion, any measure which placed Protestants on a footing of permanent equality with Roman Catholics, a position in which Protestants would (to use a common phrase) " pull only their own weight," was an offence against first principles, a measure to be resisted to the utmost, first by any arguments which came to hand, and in the last resort by other measures. They were " loyal to the Empire" but they expected loyalty from the Empire to them: placed in Ireland in a position of superiority guaranteed by the Union, they had seen the symbols of superiority one by one stripped from their shoulders. A long series of " concessions " to the Catholics (as successive steps in the establishment of religious equality were described) had, it was said, left " the Irish " without any " real grievance." The Irish were free to vote, to buy and sell, to build their churches, to have their own schools (which the State paid for), to exercise, in short, all civil rights, with the one restriction, that in the Parliament which legislated for their country they were in a permanent minority. This was the one great result, as it had been the one chief attraction, of the Union, and this it was determined at all hazards to retain.

Everybody at the time underestimated the extent and the vigour of this feeling, except those who shared it. Englishmen thought (when they heard of it) that it was all talk and that a " more reasonable view would eventually prevail": they never understood that they had rivetted upon Ireland a system which prevented its upholders from taking a " reasonable" view of anything and incapacitated them from understanding any point of view except their own. Irish Nationalists pointed to the long series of truculent threats with which Orange Ulster had greeted every measure of Irish reform. They recalled the " gun clubs" which had been the answer to the establishment of the Board of National Education: the threat to " kick the Queen's crown into the Boyne" if the Irish Church Act should be passed; and they confidently expected to see a similar luxuriance of denuncia-

## THE VOLUNTEER MOVEMENT 119

tion wither before the chilling blast of an Act of Parliament. Sinn Fein and the Republican Party (though they did not grasp the fact that what the Orange Party feared was not the suppression of their religion but the loss of its political ascendancy) adopted an attitude useless to reconcile Ulster to Home Rule but admirably calculated, once Home Rule were passed in defiance of Ulster, to work upon its feeling of resentment at the "betrayal" of its interests and exploit its wounded pride in the interests of the independence of Ireland.

But while Sinn Fein was making its proposals, unheeded (and indeed unheard) by those to whom they were addressed, to disarm the opposition of Ulster to the cause of Irish freedom, the Ulster leaders were taking steps to adopt a policy supposed to have been abandoned in Irish politics since the failure of the Fenian rising. The staid merchants, the prosperous professional classes, the sturdy farmers of Ulster, supported by the Belfast Protestant artizans, had begun to drill. Unionist Clubs were formed throughout the province: volunteers were enrolled in defiance of the law, under the pretext of being associations formed for the purpose of taking "physical exercise," though with a growing feeling of strength and security this pretext was abandoned. Talk of "guns" and "cold steel" replaced arguments based upon economic conditions and the stringency of the "bonds of Empire." A theory of "loyalty" was developed compatible with a chartered licence to defy the authority of King and Parliament in the affairs of the United Kingdom. As the inevitable day approached when, by the provisions of the Parliament Act, the Royal Assent to Home Rule must be given, the attitude of the Ulster leaders became more and more at variance with all loyal precedents. The Ulster Volunteer Force was organized as an army for service in the field: it was provided with signallers and despatch riders, with ambulance units and army nurses: hospitals were arranged to receive and tend the expected " casualties": plans were formed to seize strategic points in the province. A Provisional Government was constituted which on the day of the passing of the Act was to assume the government of Ulster and replace the King's Government until such time as it might be advisable again to restore the dispossessed monarch to his Ulster dominions. The possibility of outside alliances was not left to chance. The Volunteers were heartened by the news that " the greatest Protestant monarch" in Europe had promised his aid: the Emperor of Germany would not stand idly by while Protestantism in Ireland was put by a British Government under the heel of Irish Catholics. Rifles were still lacking, but they were not long in being supplied. They were imported from Hamburg and landed in Larne; and by means of a perfectly co-ordinated and admirable piece of organization distributed over Ulster within twenty-four hours.

All Ireland, as if stunned by the shock, waited breathlessly to see what would happen. Nothing happened. The Liberal Government, with defiance shouted in its beard, decided that, no actual breach of the "law" having been committed, no prosecutions need take place. The Cabinet was of course in a very difficult position, for it had to reckon not with the Ulster Party only but with the English Tories as well. The latter had seen from the first the uses to which the Ulster Party might be put in the English political struggle. The Conservative party hoped by exploiting "the Ulster question" to bring about the downfall of the Liberal Government: and the further the Ulster Party went, the more thoroughly they frightened moderate people in England by threats of bloodshed, anarchy and civil war, the better: the more truculent the threats of armed resistance the greater the probability that they need never be put into force. It was a dangerous game, but danger added zest to the amusement; and Irish parties, whether Unionist or Nationalist, were to English politicians persons of unaccountable vehemence whose ways were past finding out: in any case once they had served their turn they could quietly be shelved. The Cabinet seems to have considered that this alliance between the Ulster Party and the English Tories at once put the breach of the conventions of politics in Ulster under a kind of sanction and ensured that extreme action would never be taken in Ireland; for it would be absurd to assume that an English party would ever consent to the wild scheme of handing over Ulster interests to the charge of Germany; the rest would be, as it had always been, a matter of arrangement, of the expedients of which the Mother of Parliaments was still fertile. For whatever reason, then, the Cabinet decided to protest against the "unprecedented outrage" and leave the perpetrators to the judgment of posterity. But Nationalist Ireland was not inclined to see in the inaction of the Government merely the inertia of perplexed politicians waiting for an unprecedented problem to point the way to its own solution. They knew by experience that had *they* imported arms, or proclaimed their intention of doing so, or publicly flouted the meanest of the Irish Executive the Crimes Act would have been put into operation at once and his Majesty's prisons in Ireland would have been filled. They saw in the failure even to prosecute the Ulster leaders, to proclaim their organization, to deprive them of their arms, merely the traditional tenderness of the British Government to its Irish "friends." They began to believe that neither English party was really sincere in anything connected with Ireland except in the desire, whether admitted or denied, to maintain the privileges and ascendancy of the Protestant interest. Mr. Redmond was criticised with acrimony and vehemence for failing to do what he could not have done, and forcing the Cabinet to take action. When later the importation of arms into Ireland was prohibited by Order in Council, a proceeding of doubtful legality, this also was interpreted *in malam partem:* it was aimed not so much at preventing

Ulster from getting more arms as at preventing the rest of Ireland from getting any. It was a piquant situation. Ulster, which had been for a century the backbone of the "loyalist" interest in Ireland, whose one publicly proclaimed panacea for all Irish disorders and complaints had been "the firm and impartial administration of the law," which had called for the suppression of every attempt on the part of Nationalist Ireland even to express its national aspirations, was now openly contemptuous of the law, loud in its expressions of defiance of the Government and charging the Cabinet, suspected of some faint determination to do something to assert itself, with "organizing a pogrom." On the other hand Nationalist Ireland, the supposed enemy of all law, order and even public decency, was lifting up its hands in horror at the insult to the majesty of British law and calling upon its representatives in Parliament to do something, anything, to ensure respect for it. It called upon the Government to show itself to be in earnest, the Government being in reality as much in earnest as anybody. But, perplexed at the prospect of having to enforce the law in Ireland against the wrong people, the King's Government continued to eye the Ulster Government, each "willing to wound and yet afraid to strike." As a matter of fact the Ulster leaders, had they been put to the pinch, could not have made their authority really effective even in their own area: but with admirable and consummate audacity they succeeded in making the fact seem so doubtful that any attempt to suppress them appeared to be involved in serious risk.

Among the Nationalists the only section which was able to use the situation to advantage was the Republican Party. To them it seemed incredible that any Irishman should be willing to fight either for or against such a measure as Home Rule, which gave Ireland a subordinate and impoverished parliament and retained the Imperial connection practically unimpaired. But whatever the merits of the measure in itself it had in their eyes one wholly admirable result. It had for the first time since the days of the Fenians roused a section of Irishmen to arm against the British Government: and it had opened the eyes of all Irish Unionists, armed or unarmed in opposition to it, to the fact that the interests of their party, courted and promoted in Ireland for a century in English interests, were as nothing to an English Government when the exigencies of party warfare required that they should be sacrificed. Their view was put forcibly and humorously by P. H. Pearse in an article contributed to *Irish Freedom* in 1913. " It is now," he wrote, " the creed of Irish nationalism (or at least of that Irish nationalism which is vocal on platforms and in the Press) that the possession of arms and the knowledge of the use of arms is a fit subject for satire. To have a rifle is as ridiculous as to have a pimple at the end of your nose, or a bailiff waiting for you round the corner. To be able to use a rifle is an accomplishment as futile as to be able to stand on your head or to be able to wag your ears. This is not the creed of any nationalism that exists or has ever existed in any community, civilized or uncivilized, that has ever inhabited the globe. It has never been the creed of Irish nationalism until this our day. Mitchel and the great confessors of Irish nationalism would have laughed it to scorn. Mitchel indeed did laugh to scorn a similar but much less foolish doctrine of O'Connell's; and the generation that came after O'Connell rejected his doctrine and accepted Mitchel's. The present generation of Irish Nationalists is not only unfamiliar with arms but despises all who are familiar with arms. Irish Nationalists share with certain millionaires the distinction of being the only people who believe in Universal Peace—here and now. . . . It is foolish of an Orangeman to believe that his personal liberty is threatened by Home Rule: but, granting that he believes that, it is not only in the highest degree common sense, but it is his clear duty to arm in defence of his threatened liberty. Personally, I think the Orangeman with a rifle a much less ridiculous figure than the Nationalist without a rifle; and the Orangeman who can fire a gun will certainly count for more in the end than the Nationalist who can do nothing cleverer than make a pun. . . . . I am not defending the Orangeman; I am only showing that his condemnation does not lie in the mouth of an unarmed Nationalist. . . . . Negotiations might be opened with the Orangeman on these lines: You are creating a Provisional Government of Ulster—make it a Provisional Government of Ireland and we will recognize and obey it. O'Connell said long ago that he would rather be ruled by the old Protestant Ascendancy Irish Parliament than by the Union Parliament; 'and O'Connell was right,' said Mitchel. He certainly was. . . . . Any six Irishmen would be a better Government of Ireland than the English Cabinet has been. . . . . Better exploit Ireland for the benefit of Belfast than exploit her for the benefit of Westminster. A rapprochement between Orangemen and Nationalists would be difficult. The chief obstacles are the Orangeman's lack of humour and the Nationalist's lack of guns: each would be at a disadvantage in a conference. But a sense of humour can be cultivated, and guns can be purchased. One great source of misunderstanding has now disappeared: it has become clear within the last few years that the Orangeman is no more loyal to England than we are. He wants the Union because he imagines that it secures his prosperity: but he is ready to fire on the Union flag the moment it threatens his prosperity. The position is perfectly plain and understandable. Foolish notions of loyalty to England being eliminated, it is a matter for businesslike negotiation. A Nationalist mission to North-east Ulster would possibly effect some good. The case might be put thus: Hitherto England has governed Ireland through the Orange Lodges: she now proposes to govern Ireland through the A.O.H. You object: so do we. Why not unite and get rid of the English? They are the real difficulty; their presence here the real incongruity." When Pearse wrote this he seemed like a voice crying in the wilderness: but the echoes answered sooner than anyone expected. Pearse afterwards confessed that this and other articles contributed by him at this time to *Irish Freedom* were written " with the deliberate intention by argument, invective, and satire, of goading those who shared my political views to commit themselves definitely to an armed movement." The armed movement which resulted was that of the Irish Volunteers.

## ULSTER AND NATIONALIST IRELAND.

Nationalist Ireland had been officially committed to a peaceful and constitutional policy since the inception of the Home Rule Movement in 1870. Home Rule did not satisfy, and was never admitted as satisfying, the national demand. But the Fenian Movement had at last driven into the heads of even Irish landlords and Tories that some concession to national sentiment was necessary if the government of Ireland was to be made a tolerable task for decent men. The Home Rule programme was one in which Repealers and Conservatives agreed to join, the former in despair of getting anything better, the latter in despair of retaining any longer all that they had. But once accepted by the Repealers it had committed them, in the necessities of the case, to a strictly parliamentary policy; and that policy continued to be pursued even after the necessities which caused it to be adopted ceased to operate. It was not a policy ever accepted without reservation by Irish Nationalists: a considerable body of them held aloof always from the Home Rulers, regretting the old virile ways and words of Mitchel and Davis, and regarding the Home Rule programme as a Tory snare into which Irish Nationalism had fallen. The years of Parnell's leadership saw a nearer approach to national unanimity in the parliamentary policy than was seen before or has been seen since. But it was emphatically in the eyes of "strong" Nationalists a policy that could only be justified by results, and the results were slow to appear. When they appeared at last in the shape of a Home Rule Bill of the Asquith Ministry there is no doubt that had it been carried and put into operation the advocates of a stronger policy would have been overborne by the men of moderate opinions. That is not to say that Home Rule would have been accepted by all coming generations as a satisfactory solution of the Irish situation; but it would have meant an immediate settling down of the country to the solution of many internal problems and the return to Ireland of something approaching the normal conditions of a civilized country. The prospect was shattered by the enrolling of the Ulster Volunteers. To the ordinary Home Ruler, the moderate Irish Nationalist, their action seemed to be a gross and unpardonable breach of faith. For a century Irish Unionists had uttered to Irish Nationalists the unvarying challenge to acknowledge and submit to the supremacy of the Imperial Parliament: they had called upon Ireland to abandon its appeal to history and its "impossible claims" to an independence which Parliament could never sanction. The Home Rule Party had done so: no renunciation of a claim to sovereign independence could be more explicit and unequivocal than that made by Mr. Redmond. So far as the Home Rule Party

was concerned, they had agreed to all the terms
imposed upon them: they had appealed to Parliament, submitting to all the conditions implied in
the recognition of it as the court of final resort,
and now their opponents challenged in advance the
competence of Parliament to decide, and fell back
upon the weapons which Nationalist Ireland had
been persuaded to abandon. But though the
Ulster Unionists might break the pact, it was
generally expected that the court to which they
had taken their appeal would see that its competence to decide it was not challenged. The
expectation was vain. The English Tory Party
bluntly proclaimed that if Ulster decided to
repudiate the verdict of Parliament, Ulster
would be supported in any measure to that
end which it should resolve to take. And
in the face of this proclamation the Liberal Party
seemed to hesitate: the Irish Party in Parliament
could extract nothing from the Government
beyond vague assurances that all would finally be
well. Nationalist Ireland, surprised, uneasy,
suspicious, indignant saw nothing more reassuring
than broad smiles of indulgent benevolence upon
the faces of Cabinet Ministers.

But Ulster Unionists were not the only people
in Ireland who disliked Home Rule. It was just
as little to the taste of Sinn Fein and the Republicans and the Labour Party as it was to them.
If the Ulster Party thought that Home Rule was
too great a concession, the others thought that it
was practically no concession at all. But being

## ULSTER AND NATIONALIST IRELAND 131

in a minority they were prepared for the present to submit. The Sinn Fein Party and the Republicans were well aware that Home Rule meant a set back to their programme. Little as it conferred in comparison with what they wished to have, it was certain to allay for many years the sting of Irish discontent and to prolong the period during which Ireland would seek its satisfaction in the shadow of its coming fortunes. The Labour Party had already begun to organize its forces with a view to participation in the activities of the expected Parliament, and looked forward with a modest confidence to its immediate future. To all of these the arming of Ulster, which made the Parliamentarians so indignant, was a light in the darkness. They had been for years protesting unheeded against a policy which acknowledged the Act of Union by acknowledging the supremacy of the Parliament which it set up: their words had fallen for the most part upon stopped ears. And now from the party supposed to regard the supremacy of Parliament as on a level with the Ten Commandments came the mutterings of revolt and the rattle of arms. Ulster had decided to defy " the English edict which would keep Irishmen disarmed while the meanest Englishman may arm himself to the teeth"; Ulster had taken up arms " against the usurped authority of the Parliament of Great Britain to make laws to bind them." *Sinn Fein* promised that Unionist Ulster would in its coming struggle with the English Parliament " receive the sympathy and support of Nationalist

Ireland." From the Republican Party the action of the Volunteers received unstinted and enthusiastic commendation. "Ulster has done one thing," wrote *Irish Freedom*, " which commands the respect and admiration of all genuine Nationalists—she has stood up for what she believes to be right and will be cajoled neither by English threats nor English bayonets. Her attitude in this affair is the attitude of the O'Neills and the O'Donnells: no other people but an Irish people could do it and something of the kind was very necessary to shame the rest of Ireland out of J.P.-ships and jobs into some facing of the facts. . . . . In present circumstances accursed be the soul of any Nationalist who would dream of firing a shot or drawing a sword against the Ulster Volunteers in connection with this Bill. Any such action would be an enforcement of a British law upon an Irish populace which refused it, would be a marshalling under the Union Jack. We are willing to fight Ulster or to negotiate with her, but we will not fight her over the miserable shadow of autonomy, we will not fight her because she tells England to go to Hell." " The sheen of arms in Ulster was always the signal for the rest of Ireland. And Ireland even in this generation, hypnotized as most of her people are by catch cries about 'imperilling Home Rule,' by mockeries of all ' wild' politics and ' wild' plans, by doctrines even more debasing in their shameless lying than O'Connell's, Ireland has answered the call."

But to see in a revolt against a particular Act

of Parliament a revolt against the supremacy of Parliament *simpliciter* was a mistake. Ulster was willing, anxious indeed, that the supremacy of the Imperial Parliament should be maintained in Ireland, but she made one condition: that Parliament should ensure in Ireland the Protestant Ascendancy. For that Ulster Protestantism professed to be prepared to fight to the death. It was secured by the Legislative Union; and to weaken the Union was to weaken it. So long as Ireland formed "an integral part of the United Kingdom," so long as Catholic Irishmen were in a permanent minority in the Parliament of that kingdom, so long did it seem certain that the Protestant interest would be secure. Protestant England was considered to have made a pact with Protestant Ulster, and Ulster was prepared to enforce its observance even by force of arms. Ulster trembled when the shadow of the Vatican fell across her as men once trembled at an eclipse of the sun: and the Union seemed the only guarantee that recurrent eclipses would not be the harbingers of a perpetual darkness.

And whatever elements of hope for the future Sinn Fein and Republican Ireland might see in the attitude of the Ulster Volunteers towards England it was plain that while they might be praised and imitated they could not be followed. They were a strictly sectarian force formed to promote a strictly sectarian object, while Sinn Feiners and Republicans stood for the union of all Irishmen without distinction of creed. And their close (and, as it seemed to many Irishmen, unnatural) alliance with the English Tory Party was clear proof that their revolt (so far as it went) against the authority of Parliament could and would be utilized to the greater advantage of England and the detriment of Ireland. Ulster might propose to fight for her own hand and her own position in Ireland, but her English allies would see to it that nothing which Ulster gained would be lost to England. The moral to be drawn was that Ulster being part of Ireland was, however wayward and bitter, to be treated with consideration and respect; her fears for her safety to be allayed; even her prejudices to be considered and met; her incipient feeling of resentment against England applauded and encouraged. So far and no farther Irish Nationalists could go: but Ulster's claim to ascendancy could not for a moment be recognized. Meanwhile the rest of Ireland should follow the example of the North and arm in defence of a threatened liberty.

This was the attitude not merely of Sinn Feiners and Republicans, but of many followers of the Parliamentary Party. But the bulk of the parliamentarians took a different view. Some of them deprecated all appeals to violence on the part of Irish Nationalists and held that it was the business of Parliament to enforce its own authority upon the recalcitrants: others thought nothing should be done, because nothing need be done, Ulster being accustomed to threaten, but never being known to strike: others again thought that the

## ULSTER AND NATIONALIST IRELAND 135

Ulster threats should be countered by threats as determined, backed by means not less efficacious.

The last of these Nationalist sections joined with the Republicans and some of the Sinn Feiners, Sinn Fein still officially adhering to its traditional policy, to form, in imitation of the Ulstermen, the force of the Irish Volunteers. The promoters of the movement were anxious to avoid all appearance of opposition to a body of Irishmen whom, however they might differ from them and no matter what collisions with them might occur later, they respected for their vigour and resolution: on the other hand they desired to make it perfectly plain that Ulster was not the only part of Ireland that had the courage to proclaim its intention of standing up for its rights. At a meeting held in the Rotunda in Dublin on November 25, 1913, the movement was publicly inaugurated.

Of the committee which took charge of the movement during its earlier stages some were (or had been) supporters of Sinn Fein, others were Republicans, more than a third were supporters of the Parliamentary Party and a few had never identified themselves with any Irish political party of any kind. And the manifesto to the Irish people issued by the committee bore clear indications of its composite origin. It took sides neither with nor against any form of Irish Nationalism and it contained no word of hostility against the Ulster force. "The object proposed," it said, "for the Irish Volunteers is to secure and maintain the rights and liberties common to all the people of Ireland. Their duties will be defensive and protective, and they will not contemplate either aggression or domination. Their ranks are open to all able-bodied Irishmen without distinction of creed, politics or social grade. . . . In the name of National Unity, of National Dignity, of National and Individual Liberty, of Manly Citizenship, we appeal to our countrymen to recognize and accept without hesitation the opportunity that has been granted them to join the ranks of the Irish Volunteers, and to make the movement now begun not unworthy of the historic title which it has adopted." Volunteers were to sign a declaration that they desired " to be enrolled in the Irish Volunteers formed to secure and maintain the rights and liberties common to all the people of Ireland without distinction of creed, class or politics." The final words of the declaration were an answer to the charge, printed in an English newspaper a few days before, that the new movement was to form a Volunteer force of Catholics in hostility to Protestants, and an answer by anticipation to the charge, made freely afterwards, that the Volunteers were intended to deprive Unionist Ulster of her just rights. The attitude deliberately adopted towards Ulster could not have been better put than it was by the President of the Volunteers, Professor Eoin MacNeill, in his speech at the inaugural meeting. " We do not contemplate," he said, " any hostility to the Volunteer movement that has already been initiated in parts of Ulster.

The strength of that movement consists in men whose kinsfolk were amongst the foremost and the most resolute in winning freedom for the United States of America, in descendants of the Irish Volunteers of 1782, of the United Irishmen, of the Antrim and Down insurgents of 1798, of the Ulster Protestants who protested in thousands against the destruction of the Irish Parliament in 1800. The more genuine and successful the local Volunteer movement in Ulster becomes, the more completely does it establish the principle that Irishmen have the right to decide and govern their own national affairs. We have nothing to fear from the existing Volunteers in Ulster nor they from us. We gladly acknowledge the evident truth that they have opened the way for a National Volunteer movement, and we trust that the day is near when their own services to the cause of an Irish Nation will become as memorable as the services of their forefathers."

This was noble and chivalrous language and it loses none of its force when one recollects that many of the platforms in Ulster were ringing at the time with denunciations of " our hereditary enemies" and with references to Irish Catholics as " hewers of wood and drawers of water," "the men whom we hate and despise."

But in spite of the fact that the leaders of the Irish Volunteers wished to preserve, and largely succeeded in preserving, a non-provocative attitude towards the Ulstermen, the governing facts of the situation could hardly be ignored completely.

Phrases used at meetings for the enrolment of Irish Volunteers appreciative of the spirit of Ulster were strongly resented by many Nationalists who saw in the Ulster Volunteers a menace not to the English exploitation of Ireland but to the national hopes. And even the leading spirits in the movement could not conceal the fact that the Ulster Volunteers, whatever they might prove to be in the future, were certainly a present obstacle to the attainment of Home Rule, which, little regarded by Sinn Fein and the Republicans as a final settlement, was undoubtedly the only approach to a settlement that could be looked for in the near future. The blame of this it was sought to throw on the English Tory Party. "A use has been made," said Professor MacNeill, "and is daily made, of the Ulster Volunteer movement, that leaves the whole body of Irishmen no choice but to take a firm stand in defence of their liberties. The leaders of the Unionist Party in Great Britain and the journalists, public speakers and election agents of that party are employing the threat of armed force to control the course of political elections and to compel, if they can, a change of Government in England with the declared object of deciding what all parties admit to be vital political issues concerning Ireland. They claim that this line of action has been successful in recent parliamentary elections and that they calculate by it to obtain further successes, and at the most moderate estimate to force upon this country some diminished and mutilated form

## ULSTER AND NATIONALIST IRELAND 139

of National Self-Government. This is not merely to deny our rights as a nation. If we are to have our concerns regulated by a majority of British representatives owing their position and powers to a display of armed force, no matter from what quarter that force is derived, it is plain to every man that even the modicum of civil rights left to us by the Union is taken from us, our franchise becomes a mockery and we ourselves become the most degraded nation in Europe. This insolent menace does not satisfy the hereditary enemies of our National Freedom. Within the past few days a political manifesto has been issued, signed most fittingly by a Castlereagh and a Beresford, calling for British Volunteers and for money to arm and equip them to be sent into Ireland to triumph over the Irish people and to complete their disfranchisement and enslavement."

All this was true, but it was only half the truth. It was true that the Tory Party was making use of the threat of armed force; but the threat had been made before the Tory Party could make use of it, and it had been made by a body of armed Irishmen. But the followers were, as often happens, less virulent than their leaders; and months after this the sight might have been witnessed in Belfast of Ulster Volunteers and Irish Volunteers using the same drill ground through the good offices of a tolerant Ulsterman: and though the Ulster Volunteers were prepared undoubtedly to fight for their privileges, some of the most vicious appeals to their passions and their prejudices came from men who were not of the Ulster, not even of the Irish, blood. Right through their tragic and tempestuous career the Irish Volunteers in spite of countless difficulties and provocations continued their attitude of punctilious courtesy to the Ulster force. When the Ulstermen succeeded in their great coup of running a cargo of rifles from Hamburg to Larne the *Irish Volunteer* congratulated them heartily and warmly. Their attitude towards their fellow-countrymen was deeply regretted, but for what they had done to assert the freedom of Irishmen from English dictation they were accorded generous praise. The spirit of the leaders in this matter permeated the force. The head of the Irish Volunteers in Tralee wrote at a time when threats of suppressing the Ulstermen with the help of the army were made: " To my mind the Volunteers should prevent if possible and by force the English soldiers attacking the Ulster rebels. Say to the English soldiers and to the English Government, ' This is our soil and the Ulster rebels are our countrymen; fire on them and you fire on us.' . . . . Ulster is not our real enemy, though . . . . Ulster thinks we are her enemy. Time will prove who are Ulster's friends and ours."

But the history of the Irish Volunteers, though indispensable for the understanding of the development of Sinn Fein is not the history of Sinn Fein. Individual Sinn Feiners were prominent in the movement and brought into it the spirit of national unity and disregard of the

## ULSTER AND NATIONALIST IRELAND 141

differences of creed which kept Irishmen divided: but the Sinn Fein organization remained distinct, praising, warning and criticizing the new movement and the tactics of its leaders. It pointed out at once that for the Volunteers to combine and to drill was not enough: they must have rifles and rifle ranges, and urged that the provision of them should be seen to without delay. But though it wished the Volunteers to be equipped as effectively and as quickly as possible it still regarded an armed force of Irishmen as inadequate to the task of winning Irish freedom. "To help the Volunteer movement," said *Sinn Fein*, "is a national duty: they may not defeat England, but the movement will help to make Ireland self-reliant." And *Sinn Fein* was emphatic in urging the dangers of a sectional policy, of any attempt to narrow the basis upon which the new force was to be built up. "It is better," ran a leader on the subject, "at the beginning of the National Volunteer movement there should be frank speaking and frank understanding. If it were designed to be a movement confined to or controlled by any one Nationalist section we would not write a word in its support. It would fail badly. . . . . It is quite true that we must work through public opinion in the circumstances of Ireland rather than through force of arms, but it is a poor thinker who does not realize that the public opinion which lacks the confidence, the calmness, the steadiness, the judgment, the resolution and the understanding which a training in arms gives a people is a poor weapon to rely upon in times of crisis." The Volunteers were in the opinion of Sinn Fein a useful auxiliary in the task of developing the one quality from which alone ultimate success was to be expected, the self-reliance and moral resolution of the Irish people. But αὐτὸς ἐφέλκεται ἄνδρα σίδηρος—the mere "sheen of arms" has an attraction superior to all arguments and all policies: and there is little doubt that the superior attractions of the Volunteers proved too strong for many young and ardent Sinn Feiners and induced them to put the means first and the end second. The phrase of *Irish Freedom* in noticing the inauguration of the Volunteers probably gives the view of most of the younger generation: "In this welcome departure from our endless talk we touch reality at last."

The Irish Volunteers were not the only militant body which the example of Ulster had formed in Ireland. While the Ulster campaign was in full swing the workers of Dublin had been engaged in a bitter industrial struggle with their employers in which after a prolonged battle victory had somewhat doubtfully declared itself against them. The Labour leader, Jim Larkin, decided to found a Citizen Army for Irish workers. "Labour," he said in addressing the meeting at which the new force was inaugurated, "in its own defence must begin to train itself to act with disciplined courage and with organized and concentrated force. How could they accomplish this? By taking a leaf out of the book of Carson. If Carson had permission to train his braves of the North to fight against the aspirations of the Irish people, then it was legitimate and fair for Labour to organize in the same militant way to preserve their rights and to ensure that if they were attacked they would be able to give a very satisfactory account of themselves." He went on to say that the object of the Citizen Army was "that Labour might no longer be defenceless but might be able to utilize that great physical power which it possessed to prevent their elemental rights from being taken from them and to evolve such a system of unified action, self-control and ordered discipline that Labour in Ireland might march in the forefront of all movements for the betterment of the whole people of Ireland." The Citizen Army thus formed, never very numerous, efficient or enthusiastic, was practically destroyed by the formation of the Irish Volunteers. Most of its members joined the Volunteers, partly because they were the more numerous and popular body, but principally because a national policy had more attraction for them than one which was purely sectional. Captain White, who had trained the first Citizen Army, now urged that it should be reorganized upon a broader basis and in March, 1914, the Citizen Army, which afterwards played such a memorable part, was put upon its final footing. The new constitution was as follows: " That the first and last principle of the Irish Citizen Army is the avowal that the ownership of Ireland, moral and material, is vested of right in the people of Ireland: that the Irish Citizen Army shall stand for the absolute unity of Irish nationhood and shall support the rights and liberties of the democracies of all nations: that one of its objects shall be to sink all differences of birth, property and creed under the common name of the Irish People: that the Citizen Army shall be open to all who accept the principle of equal rights and opportunities for the Irish People."

It might have seemed that the constitution and principles of the Citizen Army were wide enough and national enough to justify a union or at least a close co-operation with the Irish Volunteers. But at first the two bodies held sternly aloof. The Labour Party had not been invited to send representatives to the meeting at which the Volunteers had been inaugurated, and many of the Volunteer Committee were suspected, rightly or wrongly, of being entirely out of sympathy with Labour ideals and Labour policy. When members of the Labour Party began to flock into the Volunteer ranks their action was the occasion of a bitter controversy in the official Labour organ. The Sinn Fein movement, whose spirit was supposed to preside over the Volunteer organization, had never been on cordial terms with organized Labour, and the members of the Irish Citizen Army were publicly warned to keep clear of these "Girondin politicians, who will simply use the workers as the means towards their own security and comfort." Nor were the members of the Ancient Order of Hibernians and of the United Irish League who belonged to the Volunteer Committee any more to the taste of Labour; they regarded these two bodies as bitter and implacable opponents of their rights. Regarding themselves as the true successors of the Nationalism of Wolfe Tone and John Mitchel, they called upon the Volunteers for an explicit declaration of what was meant by " the rights common to all Irishmen " which they were enrolled to maintain. Did they mean the right to Home Rule, or to the constitution of 1782 or to an Irish Republic? The Volunteers could not have said " Yes " to any one of the three alternatives without driving out members who desired to say " Yes " to one or other of the remaining two. The Volunteers had deliberately left in abeyance controversies which the Labour Army wished to fight out in advance. They, undoubtedly, desired a Republic and meant to say so. When it was announced that the Irish Volunteers would be under the control of the Irish Parliament (when there should be such a body to control them) Labour became more suspicious still; was not the only Irish Parliament even in contemplation to be subordinate to the Parliament of England? The Volunteers seemed to treat the Citizen Army with indifference, if not with contempt: and a bitter antagonism was developed which only common misfortune was able to mitigate.

In all this welter of sharp antagonisms and conflicting policies the only party which walked in the old political ways was the Parliamentary Party. They expected confidently that political conventions would finally be observed or that Parliament would deal effectively with those who tried to break them. It was becoming plain, however, as time went on that the conventions were not going to be regarded and that Parliament was as likely as not to acquiesce in the breach of them. And the Party was not aware of the change that was slowly passing over Ireland. A long tenure of their place among the great personages and amid the high doings of Westminster seemed to have made them somewhat oblivious of the fact that Irish politics are made in Ireland. They did not feel the thrill of chastened pride that shivered gently through Ireland when the quiet places of Ulster echoed to the march of the Ulster Volunteers. They did not know how many Irishmen regarded the action of Ulster not as a menace to the dignity of the Parliament in which the Party sat but as the harbinger of national independence. They underrated (as who then did not?) the influence of Sinn Fein; they regarded the foundation of the Irish Volunteers as the work of "irresponsible young men," though the "young men" were nearer the heart of Young Ireland: like O'Connell, they "stood for Old Ireland and had some notion that Old Ireland would stand by them." Ireland, though no one guessed it at the time, was the crucible in which were slowly melting and settling down all the elements that were to go to the making of the future Sinn Fein.

Sinn Fein was at the time to all outward seeming an insignificant and discredited party with an

ULSTER AND NATIONALIST IRELAND 147

impossible programme. It still published a small weekly paper with no great circulation. It did not agree with the parliamentarians: it had a standing feud with the Labour Party: it gave a dignified and pontifical blessing to the Volunteers without committing itself to their whole programme. Its only electioneering venture, outside municipal politics, had been a disastrous failure: it had won a few seats on the Dublin City Council: it had tried and failed to run a daily paper. When all Nationalist Ireland was waiting for Home Rule it declared Home Rule to be a thing of naught. To the buoyant confidence of the Parliamentary Party it opposed a cynical distrust of their aims and methods, a constant incredulity of their ultimate success. When the Party pointed to what it had done and to what it was about to do, Sinn Fein reminded the country that the very existence of a Parliamentary Party was an acknowledgment of the Act of Union. When the Liberal Government was engaged in an embittered and apparently final struggle for supremacy with the Tory Party in the interests of Ireland, Sinn Fein professed entire disbelief in its sincerity; it asserted that the Liberals really loved the Tories very much better than they loved the Irish. With a querulous and monotonous insistence it preached distrust of all English parties and even of the English nation, towards whom it displayed a hostility that seemed almost to amount to a monomania. To Irish Labour this indiscriminating attitude seemed insensate bigotry: to the Irish

people as a whole it seemed incomprehensible that
a Nationalist Party should regard the Liberals
as enemies and the Ulster Volunteers as brothers
in arms. Sinn Fein never seemed less certain of
a future in Ireland than when events were preparing to make Ireland Sinn Fein.

Early in 1914 *Sinn Fein* saw in the King's
Speech at the opening of Parliament indications
that the Cabinet and the Opposition had arranged
" a deal" over Home Rule and foretold an attempt
at compromise. The next month the Prime
Minister proposed the partition of Ireland between
the Unionists and the Nationalists and the Irish
Party accepted the proposal as a temporary device
to ease the parliamentary situation for the Cabinet.
No proposal better calculated to offend the deepest
instincts of Irish nationalism could have been
made: no concession more fatal to the party which
agreed to it could have been devised. The mention
of it provoked an outburst in Ireland which did
more to smash the Parliamentary Party and leave
the field open to their rivals than anything which
had happened since Home Rule was first mooted.
The criticisms passed upon it by the non-Parliamentary Nationalists were important, not so much
on account of the quarters they came from, as for
the grounds on which they were made, and their
words awakened deeper feelings than had come to
the surface for years. " To even discuss," said
*Sinn Fein*, " the exclusion of Ulster or any portion of Ulster from a Home Rule measure is in
itself traitorous. When God made this country,

He fixed its frontiers beyond the power of man to alter while the sea rises and falls. . . . . So long as England is strong and Ireland is weak, England may continue to oppress this country, but she shall not dismember it." "If this nation is to go down," wrote *Irish Freedom*, " let it go down gallantly as becomes its history, let it go down fighting, but let it not sink into the abjectness of carving a slice out of itself and handing it over to England. . . . As for Ulster, Ulster is Ireland's and shall remain Ireland's. Though the Irish nation in its political and corporate capacity were gall and wormwood to every Unionist in Ulster yet shall they swallow it. We will fight them if they want fighting: but we shall never let them go, never." Sinn Fein and the Republicans were no more emphatic than the Labour Party. James Connolly in the *Irish Worker* said of Partition: " To it Labour should give the bitterest opposition, against it Labour in Ulster should fight even to the death if necessary as our fathers fought before us." It even used the menace of partition as an argument in favour of joining the Citizen Army and urged that Volunteers should transfer their membership to a body which " meant business." " The Citizen Army," said an article signed with the initials of one of its principal organizers, " stands for Ireland —Orange and Green—one and indivisible. The men who tread the valleys and places Cuchullain, Conall Cearnach, Russell and McCracken trod are bone of our bone and flesh of our flesh. Because they may have a different creed does not matter to us; it never mattered to the Government: an Irish Protestant corpse dangled as often at the end of a rope as did the corpse of an Irish Catholic."

But Sinn Fein saw that, though partition was unacceptable, it was no use continually asking the Ulstermen to name the safeguards they wanted. They would not name what they did not want: no safeguards would secure them in a democratic modern community against their chief objection to Home Rule—that in an Irish Parliament Protestants, as such, would be in " a permanent minority." It was of the very nature of things that they should be, if representative institutions were to be recognized at all. But though in a minority they need not be, as they asserted they would be, subject to disabilities, and Sinn Fein held that every offer to allay their fears compatible with free institutions should be made. A Sinn Fein Convention held in Dublin towards the end of April, 1914, agreed to make the Ulstermen, on behalf of Sinn Fein, the following proposals: (1), increased representation in the Irish Parliament on the basis partly of population, partly of rateable value and partly of bulk of trade, the Ulster representation to be increased by fifteen members including one for the University of Belfast: two members to be given to the Unionist constituency of Rathmines; (2), to fix all Ireland as the unit for the election of the Senate or Upper House and to secure representation to the Southern Unionist minority by Proportional Representation; (3), to

## ULSTER AND NATIONALIST IRELAND 151

guarantee that no tax should be imposed on the linen trade without the consent of a majority of the Ulster representatives; (4), that the Chairman of the Joint Exchequer Board should always be chosen by the Ulster Representatives; (5), that all posts in the Civil Service should be filled by examination; (6), that the Ulster Volunteer Force should be retained under its present leaders as portion of an Irish Volunteer Force and should not, except in case of invasion, be called upon to serve outside Ulster; (7), that the Irish Parliament should sit alternately in Dublin and in Belfast; (8), that the clauses in the Home Rule Bill restricting Irish trade and finance and prohibiting Ireland from collecting and receiving its own taxes, or otherwise conflicting with any of the above proposals, should be amended. These proposals, the most statesmanlike and generous proposals put forward on the Nationalist side, were, though approved of generally by the Belfast Trades Council, contemptuously ignored by the Ulster leaders.

The offer of partition likewise was promptly rejected by Ulster: like the Irish Citizen Army they "meant business." They meant to smash Home Rule for good and all, for the South as well as for the North of Ireland, and in conjunction with the English Tories they felt strong enough to do it. They began openly to tamper with the allegiance of the army. Nor were their efforts without success. Not only did large numbers of ex-officers offer their services to the Ulster

Volunteers, but many officers upon the active list announced their intention of refusing to obey orders if despatched to preserve order in Ulster and forestall the intention, broadly hinted, of some of the Ulstermen to seize military depots in the province. It was an open boast in Belfast that the ship conveying the arms from Hamburg to Ulster had been sighted, but allowed to pass unchallenged by officers of the Royal Navy on the ships detailed to intercept it. They seemed deliberately to have adopted the policy of Catiline, *ruina exstinguere incendium*, " to put out the fire by pulling down the house." If the Protestant interest were to go down in Ireland, then should the British Constitution which had fostered it go down with it.

All this was, of course, matter for unfeigned delight to all the "advanced" people both in Ireland and outside of it. If officers were to have the option of obeying orders or not at their will why should a like latitude be denied the common soldier? If officers refused to act against Ulster why should a private be required to fire upon strikers? Thanks were publicly returned by *Irish Freedom* to " the gallant British officers who have helped their beloved Empire on to the brink above the precipice." But so far as England was concerned, the crisis was tided over by the usual method of compromise. There had been a " misunderstanding" for which both sides were more or less responsible. There had been no actual intention of employing force in a political dispute and therefore the question in debate did not arise.

The Minister of War was dismissed on a side issue, the Premier assumed his responsibilities and everybody was more or less satisfied, except the Irish.

Whatever were the rights or wrongs of the dispute between the Army and the Government, it was plain that the dispute had been composed at the expense of Home Rule. Partition in some form or other was now certain to accompany Home Rule, if Home Rule were not actually shelved. The Irish Party were solemnly warned by the advanced Nationalist papers. "Mr. Redmond has had his chance," wrote one of these. "When partition is again mentioned, let him stand aside even at the cost of the 'Home Rule' Bill. There is a force and a spirit growing in Ireland which in the wrangle of British politics he but vaguely realizes."

But Mr. Redmond was not so preoccupied with "the wrangle of British politics" as he seemed. He realized quite clearly that the Irish Volunteers were growing in numbers and in influence and that neither their object nor their existence was compatible with the principles of Home Rule. They proclaimed their intention of putting themselves eventually at the disposal of the Irish Parliament: but the Bill contemplated a Parliament which should have no right to accept their services. They were largely controlled by men who thought little of Home Rule and everything of the "rights of Irishmen," which might mean just what the Liberal Government proposed to give but might

also mean a great deal more. They were a menace
to the success of the parliamentary policy, and it
seemed to be his plain duty to suppress or to
control them. To attempt suppression would be
dangerous: to control them seemed not impossible.
He decided to demand the right to nominate on
their committee twenty-five " tried and true "
Nationalists whose allegiance to his policy was
unquestioned. The committee, faced by the alternative of either declaring war on Mr. Redmond
(a course as dangerous to them as to declare war
on them would have been to him) or of submitting
to his demand, decided to submit. The twenty-
five new members (four of whom were priests and
the majority of the remainder Dublin Nationalists)
joined the Committee and the Irish " military
crisis" seemed to have been solved. In reality it
was only beginning. The Citizen Army promptly
declared war upon the reconstituted Volunteer
Committee. " Is there," asked *The Irish
Worker*, "one reliable man at the head of the
National Volunteer movement apart from Casement who, we believe, is in earnest and honest?
. . . . We admit the bulk of the rank and
file are men of principle and men who are out for
liberty for all men: but why allow the foulest
growth that ever cursed this land (the Hibernian
Board of Erin) to control an organization that
might if properly handled accomplish great
things." It accused the committee of having
passed the Volunteers over to a " gang of place-
hunters and political thugs" and called upon the

## ULSTER AND NATIONALIST IRELAND 155

rank and file to sever all connection with them: " Our fathers died that we might be free men. Are we going to allow their sacrifices to be as naught? Or are we going to follow in their footsteps at the Rising of the Moon?" The Citizen Army was gradually coming round to a standpoint more and more national, and saw in the control of the Volunteers by the Parliamentarians nothing but disaster to its idea of what nationalism involved. *Sinn Fein* was equally vehement: " Redmond is only a tool," it wrote, " in the hands of Asquith and Birrell who wish to destroy the Volunteers as Lord Northington was a tool in the hands of Fox, to whom he wrote in 1783: ' They have got too powerful, and there is nothing for us but for our friends to go into their meetings and disturb the harmony of them and create division.' " When Mr. Redmond appealed to America for money to " strengthen" the Volunteers it pointed out that if he had been in earnest he would have asked not for money but for arms, and would have had the Arms Proclamation withdrawn by the Government. It printed a series of letters to the Volunteers, of which the first contained the words: " The object [*i.e.* of the Volunteers] is obtaining and maintaining the independence of Ireland. Those who are in earnest should have their own committee, independent of Redmond and Co." *Irish Freedom* headed its leader on the transaction " The Kiss of Judas," and declared that " after the British Government the Irish Parliamentary Party in its later years has been the most evil force in Ireland."

The original members of the Volunteer Committee were clearly uneasy and tried to put the best face they could upon the matter. In their official organ, *The Irish Volunteer*, they informed the public " The control of the committee by Mr. John Redmond does not matter, provided his nominees represent the feelings of the Volunteers: if they do the Irish Party will see to the withdrawing of the Arms Proclamation and proceed to arm the Volunteers at once." But the Irish Party did neither; and if Mr. Redmond was expected to share the feelings of the Volunteers, the Volunteers cannot have shared the feelings of the committee. A month before this the *Irish Volunteer* had printed the following: " For over a generation Ireland has taken her national views from men whose whole lives were bound up with the preservation of the peace. Suddenly, in a day, in an hour, the whole situation has undergone a change. Force has reappeared as a factor in Irish political life. . . . . It is to be hoped that men are not joining the national army from any motives but those which actuated the founders. The object of the Volunteers is to maintain and preserve the rights and liberties common to the whole people of Ireland. There is no question of preserving merely the ' legal ' rights graciously permitted us by a foreign power." If the original committee seriously expected Mr. Redmond and his nominees to acquiesce in the views expressed in the last sentence they must have been simple to a degree. They were admittedly in a difficult position; but they knew what they meant and they knew what Mr. Redmond meant; and the sequel might have been foreseen.

It was put upon record later by a member of the committee that in the task of arming the Volunteers the new members gave little effective assistance, and that when arms were obtained they tried to have them taken from the men who had paid for them and handed over *gratis* to the Hibernians of the North to use (without, it is true, a supply of ammunition) to overawe the aggression of the Ulster Volunteers. But the members of the original committee procured arms upon their own responsibility. In July they succeeded in imitating the exploit of the Ulstermen at Larne. They ran a cargo of rifles into Howth and another was landed at Kilcool. But the forces of the Crown, absent at Larne and inactive in Ulster ever since, displayed their unsuccessful vigour at Howth. The Volunteers were intercepted on the way back, but after a scuffle succeeded in getting away with their guns. The soldiers on the return journey fired upon a provoking but unarmed crowd in the streets of Dublin. The country had barely time to appreciate the contrast between Larne and Howth, when the sound of the German guns in Belgium broke upon its ears.

## SINN FEIN, 1914—1916.

John Mitchel had prophesied that " in the event of a European war a strong national party could grasp the occasion" in Ireland, and Mitchel held too high a place in the estimation of Irish Nationalists for his words to have been forgotten or ignored. When Saurin (who, though an Orangeman and a Tory and, after the Union, one of the law officers of the Crown in Ireland, opposed the policy of Castlereagh) uttered his famous dictum on the validity of the Act of Union, he provided Irish Nationalism with one of its most authoritative maxims: "You may make the Union binding as a law, but you cannot make it obligatory in conscience: it will be obeyed as long as England is strong, but resistance to it will be in the abstract a duty and the exhibition of that resistance will be a mere question of prudence." Irish Separatists did not always find it prudent to speak with the precision of the future Attorney-General: but the principle which he laid down was always understood to be one of which they acknowledged the validity. It had been repeated in language less classical, but equally emphatic, by Parnell and Mr. Redmond; but the occasion to put into practice the prudence of which Saurin spoke had either never come or never been seized. But that it would come some day and in an unquestionable shape was a maxim of the Separatists. The increasing signs of antagonism between England and Germany had not since the beginning of the century escaped watchful eyes in Ireland. In the year 1900 *The United Irishman* in discussing German diplomacy had referred to the alliance between Irish and Germans in the United States which (it added) " is such a welcome feature of contemporary politics." When, two years before the war, Mr. Churchill had referred in guarded language to the necessity to England of a " loyal Ireland" in the near future, *Sinn Fein* commented as follows on his words: " We have, for instance, no illusion whatever on the subject of Germany. If Germany victorious over England comes to Ireland, Germany will come to stay and rule the Atlantic from our shores. She will give us better terms than England offers. She will give us that Home Rule which all the States of the German Empire enjoy. . . . . . We have no doubt whatever that Ireland under German rule would be more prosperous than she has ever been under the rule of England. . . . The fact would not induce us to love Germany or to fight for a mere change of masters. But as a matter of bargaining we can say to Mr. Churchill, when he offers us a bogus Home Rule for aiding British policy against Germany, that Ireland would get better terms from a successful Germany if she withheld that aid." This was the language of a journal which voiced the opinions of a party definitely committed against an Irish policy of force: the Republican Party, not so committed, used words less nebulous and guarded. In 1911 *Irish Freedom* printed a letter from John Devoy of New York, a prominent Irish-American and ex-Fenian, pointing out that a German war was coming in the near future, that England would need conscription before it was over, and that Ireland must fight either for England or against her. A month or so later an editorial returned to the point: " Wolfe Tone, though he appealed to France for aid, did not ask Irishmen to sit idly by; and the arguments Tone advanced with considerable success to induce France to aid in establishing an Irish Republic can be applied to-day in the case of Germany." Later in the year an article entitled " When Germany fights England " discussed the policy of Ireland, having first stipulated for her complete independence, throwing her weight on the side of Germany in a war. Germany, it was thought, might play the same part as Tone had hoped that France would play in 1798—might release Ireland from English domination and then declare her absolute independence. No doubt seems to have been entertained that such a policy would be acceptable to Germany; for in Germany the Separatists saw, not an ambitious empire grasping at world power, so much as a brave and efficient people trying to burst the bonds with which English policy and English intrigue had surrounded them. Sinn Fein had taken its official economic policy from the German List, and pointed to its success in establishing German industry upon a sure footing (in spite of the industrial rivalry of England) as an augury for Irish success and as a model for Irish effort. Germany was looked upon as the one European nation at once bold enough and strong enough to challenge English supremacy and vitally interested in challenging it effectively. For, with Ireland in the possession of England, the key to the Atlantic was in English hands: if Ireland were independent then the key would go to whatever hands framed the most favourable alliance with Ireland.

But whatever the wisdom or the folly of such expectations, there is no doubt that the Separatists looked to Germany not to annex but to free Ireland. They did not desire that Germany should take Ireland from England; but that Germany should declare Ireland to be an independent sovereign State. Nothing less than this could have satisfied their aspirations. For Germany to have offered less would not have secured their assistance; if Germany had annexed Ireland they would have welcomed a deliverer from Germany as eagerly as a deliverer was looked for then from the domination of England.

But in the actual circumstances that accompanied the outbreak of war in 1914 there was no disposition to take sides with Germany on the merits, or to stake everything upon the success of an understanding with Germany. It is true that the official statement of the English case for the declaration of war was received with a certain degree of quiet scepticism. The commercial rivalry

of the two empires, the prophecies of a coming war
that had been openly made for years, the *Entente
Cordiale* with the French Republic, of the real
meaning of which France at least made no secret,
had been too well known and had been too openly
and too long canvassed for the violation of Belgian
neutrality by Germany to receive the importance
which was attributed to it or to be regarded as
much more than a blunder adroitly utilized.
There was not so much sympathy with Germany
as a want of sympathy with England: there was
not so much a lack of sympathy with Belgium as
a distrust of the appeals which were insistently
made to that feeling.

When war was declared the Home Rule Bill
had not passed into law. A great effort had been
made to come to terms with the Ulster and the
English Tory Parties and had failed. It seemed
as if the Government must either go forward with
its policy and take the risks or own defeat. It
was assumed as a matter of course that a foreign
war ended *ipso facto* all disputes between the great
English parties and that till the war should be
over internal opposition to the Government should
cease. But what about Ireland? Would the two
Irish parties sink their differences in the same way
in the interest of the Empire? Would the Irish
people give their whole-hearted support and sympathy in the struggle to an England which had
so far failed to satisfy what they regarded as their
elementary rights? The choice fell to Mr. Redmond. On the one hand prudence counselled the

use of a unique opportunity: he might offer Irish support in return for the immediate enactment of Home Rule and throw upon the Ulster Party the onus of refusing to support the Empire in its deadly struggle. He might on the other hand offer Irish support without conditions and leave the satisfaction of the national claims of Ireland as a debt of honour to the conscience of English statesmen. Had he bargained (and got his terms) Nationalist Ireland would have been with him almost to a man: with that simplicity of character, which, as the Greek historian says, "makes up a great part of good breeding," he promised without conditions: England might withdraw her soldiers from Ireland; the shores of Ireland, North and South, would be guarded by her armed sons. The House of Commons, England and the Empire were greatly impressed: the *beau geste* of the Irish leader was universally applauded. The Home Rule Bill was presented for the Royal Signature and signed; a Suspensory Bill was hurried through providing that its operation should be postponed; the Prime Minister promised the enemies of Home Rule that before it was allowed to be put into operation the Government would introduce and pass a Bill amending the measure in such a way as to make it acceptable to its opponents; and Mr. Redmond hurried home to rally Ireland to the cause of the Empire. The situation was summed up later with brutal frankness by a Belfast Unionist paper: "If the Nationalists will not enlist because the war is just, they should not do so because they have got Home Rule; because they have not got it. The Unionist Party has declared that when it comes into power it will not allow the Act to stand." Even so between 40,000 and 50,000 Irish Nationalists joined the Forces during the first year of the war.

By the time Mr. Redmond had returned to Ireland the attitude of all Irish parties to the war had become pretty clearly defined. The Ulster Volunteers, after about a month's hesitation on the part of their leaders, had received official intimation that they were free to enlist. Any delay there may have been was due, not to the feelings of the rank and file, but to the tactics of the politicians, eager to extract the last possible advantage from the situation. The bulk of the Nationalists, like the bulk of the Ulstermen, were in sympathy with the cause of England and her Allies as against Germany and the two parties sent recruits in almost equal numbers. The attitude of Sinn Fein is put so clearly in a leader in its official organ that it deserves quotation: " Ireland is not at war with Germany: it has no quarrel with any Continental Power. . . . There is no European Power waging war against the people of Ireland: there are two European Powers at war with the people who dominate Ireland from Dublin Castle. . . . . . To-day the Irish are flattered and caressed by their libellers. England wants our aid and Mr. Redmond, true to his nature, rushes to offer it—for nothing. . . . . If England wins this war she will be more powerful than she has been at any time since 1864 and she will treat the Ireland which kissed the hand that smote her as such an Ireland ought to be treated. If she loses the war, and Ireland is foolish enough to identify itself with her, Ireland will deservedly share in her punishment. . . . . We are Irish Nationalists and the only duty we have is to stand for Ireland's interests, irrespective of the interests of England or Germany or any foreign country. . . . . Let it (*i.e.* the Government) withdraw the present abortive Home Rule Bill and pass . . . . a full measure of Home Rule and Irishmen will have some reason to mobilize for the defence of their institutions. At present they have none. In the alternative let a Provisional Government be set up in Dublin by Mr. Redmond and Sir Edward Carson and we shall give it allegiance. But the confidence trick has been too often played upon us to deceive us again. If the Irish Volunteers are to defend Ireland they must defend it for Ireland under Ireland's flag and under Irish officers. Otherwise they will only help to perpetuate the enslavement of their country. . . . . Germany is nothing to us in herself, but she is not our enemy. Our blood and our miseries are not upon her head. But who can forbear admiration at the spectacle of the Germanic people whom England has ringed round with enemies standing alone, undaunted and defiant against a world in arms?" This was a clear declaration of neutrality coupled with an offer of terms of friendship. But as the negotiations in

Parliament proceeded, as it became clear that, while Home Rule was nominally to be passed, no effect was to be given to it for the present, and no permanent validity to attach to the passing of it, the tone of the Sinn Fein and Republican Press grew harder. " If the Home Rule Bill," said *Sinn Fein*, " be signed, but not brought into immediate operation by the appointment of a Home Rule Executive Government, Ireland is sold and betrayed. Let every Irishman get that into his head and keep it there." " We regard no enemy of England as an enemy of ours. . . . . It was Grattan, the greatest of our constitutional leaders, who declared that if the interests of the Empire clashed with the liberties of Ireland, then he and every Irishman would say ' Live Ireland—perish the Empire.' " *Irish Freedom* which printed in capitals across its pages mottoes such as " Germany is not Ireland's enemy," " Ireland First, Last and All the Time," said, " If England withdraws her troops utterly from Ireland the Irish Volunteers will take and hold the country, hold it not alone against Germany but against anybody else who attempts to interfere with it. And on no other conditions will the Volunteers consent to move a step. . . . . We are not prepared to buy even freedom—were it offered—at the price of our honour." It declared that " the psychological moment" had arrived for the union of Irishmen, for the attainment of Irish liberty, and proposed for the last time a working arrangement between the Irish Volunteers and the Ulster

Volunteers to further the real liberties of Ireland. The Labour paper was even more outspoken. It ridiculed the parliamentary leaders for their lack of ability in driving a bargain as compared with the more astute Ulstermen; it ridiculed the advanced Nationalists who still talked nonsense about a junction of the two forces of Volunteers: it declared stoutly, "If England wants an Empire, let her hold the Empire. . . . . Let no Irishman leave his own land. . . . . Keep your guns for your real enemies." While it deplored the success of the recruiting campaign it allowed (with, considering its own strongly expressed views, a commendable toleration) articles to appear from Labour men giving their reasons for supporting the war. But it had no illusions as to what was in store in the end for Irishmen who put its ideas into practice. "For some of us," James Connolly wrote, "the finish may be on the scaffold, for some in the prison cell, for others more fortunate upon the battlefield of an Ireland in arms for a real republican liberty." But as a last resort even Connolly proposed terms of accommodation: he thought that the Volunteers by the bold policy of refusing to move until their terms were conceded might force the Government to repeal all clauses in the Home Rule Bill denying to Ireland the self-government enjoyed by Canada and Australia. The last number of his paper bore the legend "We serve neither King nor Kaiser." It had been decided by all the political parties that then seemed to count in Ireland that Irishmen must serve, if they served at all, not because they had been given Home Rule but because they had not been given it—because Ireland was still an integral part of the United Kingdom, bound to its fortunes till the issue of the war should be determined. Three months after war was declared the Sinn Fein, Republican and Labour papers were suppressed by the police.

The public discussion of the terms upon which it might have been possible to range even Separatists against Germany, the granting to Ireland of something of her own to defend, being thus declared not to be in the public interest, it seemed as if no obstacle remained in the way of raising recruits all over the country. Irishmen were credited with a love of mingling in a fight without any nice discrimination as to the grounds of the quarrel or the merits of the dispute. " Is there not wars?" seemed to some of the authorities to be a sufficiently potent appeal. But it was found that there existed a confused and vague feeling that England as a whole had at last, in spite of much English opposition, come to take a friendly view of the Irish claim to self-government; that, if the war had not occurred when it did, some way out of the difficulty would have been found; that the Government was honest in its intentions and could hardly be blamed for the tactics of its opponents. Even a slight and doubtful indication of real friendliness on the part of England raises in Ireland a response which must often seem to be out of proportion to the cause

which excited it; and at the beginning of the war
Nationalist Ireland was ready to respond to the
call for men in a way which roused the cynical
criticism of the advanced wing of the Nationalist
Party. "No English city," wrote the *Irish
Worker* in September, 1914, "is displaying more
enthusiasm than Dublin in sending its bravest and
best to murder men with whom they have no
quarrel." The Scottish Borderers, leaving for the
Front, received an enthusiastic send-off from the
city in which a short while before they had had
to be confined to barracks; all over the country
men were flocking to recruit in the first few weeks
of the war. Anti-English feeling was practically
smothered in a wave of enthusiasm. The Irish
Volunteers, now apparently under the assured
control of the Parliamentary Party, became the
subjects of an almost embarrassing interest.
Unionist peers and gentry, retired militia officers
and other people, not (to say the least) distinguished for Irish patriotism, hastened to enrol in
their ranks and to proffer their services. The
name of Major the Earl of Fingall appearing as
Chief Inspecting Officer of the Irish Volunteers in
Meath in an order signed by Colonel Maurice
Moore, "Inspector-General, Irish Volunteers,"
would have seemed strange six months before and
stranger still a year afterwards. But it provoked
little comment in August, 1914. It seemed as if
a miracle were about to happen and it became the
apparent business of the authorities to take steps
to secure that it should not happen.

Enlistment had not been growing in popularity in Ireland for some years before the war. In 1908, *Sinn Fein* had pointed out with satisfaction that the army returns showed that the number of Irishmen in the regular army had then fallen to the lowest point upon record. The Boer War and the anti-recruiting propaganda in Ireland had not been without their effect upon Irish feeling and the real position and work of the army in Ireland had been closely scrutinized. "The Curragh Mutiny" had provoked some very pointed comments upon the spirit which really animated the army in Ireland: it came to be looked upon as the citadel and symbol of all the forces that opposed the claims of Ireland. "We all know in our hearts," said Roger Casement and Eoin MacNeill in a manifesto published in April, 1914, in the *Irish Volunteer*, "that the 'Union'' means the military occupation of Ireland as a conquered country: that the real headquarters of Irish government on the Unionist principle is the Curragh Camp to which the offices of Dublin Castle are only a sort of vermiform appendix." And the functions performed by the army in Ireland would certainly have seemed strange to anyone who felt any attachment to the views generally accepted in England as to the relation of the army to the civil power. In the General Orders for the guidance of the troops affording aid to the Civil Power in Ireland, issued in 1891, the following paragraph is to be found: "All officers in command of corps or detachments are to transmit to the Deputy Adjutant General an immediate report of any outrages, large meetings held or expected to be held for political or other purposes, or occurrences that may take place in the neighbourhood of their posts connected with the state of the country, whether they have or have not been called upon to afford assistance to the civil power." The functions of an army acting upon instructions like these are hardly to be distinguished from those of an army of occupation, and Nationalist Ireland was well aware of the efficiency with which these functions were performed. To make enlistment popular in Ireland, even in a moment of enthusiasm, was thus a work requiring a certain amount of tact and discretion.

The first real difficulty arose with the Volunteers, whose services as an army of defence had been pledged by Mr. Redmond to the Government. The pledge had been given without the consent, or even the knowledge, of the Volunteer Committee and they resented the implication that they could be disposed of as if they were the private property of other people. They had been enrolled with a definite object and any duty for which their services were to be given must be shown to be at least not inconsistent with that object. The committee, however, so far endorsed Mr. Redmond's offer as to pass a resolution declaring " the complete readiness of the Irish Volunteers to take joint action with the Ulster Volunteer Force for the defence of Ireland." The Prime Minister promised in Parliament that the Secretary for War would " do everything in his power, after consultation with gentlemen in Ireland, to arrange for the full equipment and organization of the Irish Volunteers." Whether the powers of the Secretary for War were less extensive than the Prime Minister believed, or whether the "gentlemen in Ireland" had other views, the scheme drawn up by General Sir Arthur Paget and his staff " by which the War Office may be supplied from the Irish Volunteers with a force for the defence of Ireland" was rejected by the War Office. This, it is true, made little difference in the end, for the Volunteer Committee, when the scheme was submitted to them, demanded the inclusion of certain "primary conditions" which it was not at all likely that the War Office would have accepted: but the immediate rejection of it by the military authorities in England is significant of the spirit in which the question of Irish recruiting was approached. It was hostile not only to Irish ideals but to Irish sentiment, to everything except the use to which Irish soldiers might be put. The contrast between the treatment accorded to Irish Nationalist recruits and the privileges granted to the Ulster Division can only be explained on the assumption that the War Office desired to show appreciation of the latter and suspicion of the former. The Ulster men were allowed to retain their own officers and their own tests of admission: the "regiments" formed under the Provisional Government of Ulster were taken over, without alteration, by the English authorities: they were allowed to refuse Catholics or Nationalists who offered to enlist in their ranks: their recruiting marches were accompanied by bands who played Orange party tunes through Catholic and Nationalist hamlets while they went through the farce of lecturing the inhabitants on their " duty to the Empire in this crisis." In November, 1914, an advertisement appeared in the Dublin *Evening Mail* announcing that a new Dublin Company of the Royal Irish Fusiliers was to be formed to which none but Unionists were admissible, intending recruits being directed to apply at the Orange Hall. The Ulster Force was trained as a body in camps of its own, while Ulster Nationalists had to take train for the South or were shipped to England. Similar privileges were bluntly and persistently refused to the Nationalists. The Ulstermen had their own banners: the Nationalists might not fight under any emblem but the Union Jack, the symbol of the defeat of their nationality, of the very Act of Union against which they were known to be in protest. Treatment such as this could have only one result: the people who decided upon it must have known what the result would be, and by persisting in it showed that the result was desired. By cooling down the enthusiasm of Nationalist Ireland they made it possible to declare that Nationalist Ireland was " disappointing expectations" and to hint that they had suspected all along that it was less eager to fight than had appeared. Incidentally the result was held to justify the suspicions which had brought it about. Irish

## 174 THE EVOLUTION OF SINN FEIN

soldiers were divided into two categories: those whom the authorities delighted to honour and those whom they decided to employ. It must be added that these manufactured animosities faded away in the stress of battle. Ulstermen and Nationalists fighting side by side covered themselves with glory and did equal credit to the old land; and no more stringent criticisms of the treacherous and malignant policy that divided them can be heard than from the lips of some of the men who survived the glorious ordeal of the Somme.

But an influential body had from the first decided that the duty of Irishmen, and especially of Irish Volunteers, was to remain in Ireland; these were the members of the original Volunteer Committee and their adherents: outside the Volunteer ranks they were supported by Sinn Fein, the Republican Party and the Citizen Army. To them the supreme and immediate duty of Irishmen, and in a special degree of the Volunteers, was to safeguard the liberties of Ireland—a duty to which the fact of a European war was irrelevant, except in so far as it might afford an opportunity to strengthen and secure Irish liberty. There is little doubt that some members of this party hoped that Germany would be victorious, not in the interests of Germany but in the interests of Ireland, which had little prospect of winning concessions from an England rendered invincible by the overthrow of her most formidable rival some of them regarded the war as a mere struggle for commercial supremacy in which Ireland had no interest at stake: but they would all alike have defended the shores of Ireland against a German army which invaded them for the purposes of annexation and conquest. To all alike the proposition that Irishmen had any duty to enlist for foreign service in the English army was a denial of the very fundamental article of their creed. When Mr. Redmond, then, in his address to the Volunteers at Woodenbridge in September, 1914, urged them to enlist for service overseas the inevitable crisis was provoked. But the original provisional committee were now in a minority in the counsels of the organization they had founded, and they were hampered by a fundamental (and, indeed, intentional) ambiguity in the Volunteer pledge. "The rights and liberties common to all Irishmen" was not a phrase which carried its interpretation on its face. It was open to the Volunteer followers of Mr. Redmond to say that the democracy of Great Britain had conferred upon Ireland a "charter of liberty" and that it was the duty of Irishmen to fight for Great Britain, keeping faith with those who had kept faith with them. It was open to others to say that "the Thing on the Statute Book" fell far short of conferring upon Irishmen the rights and liberties to which they were entitled, and that the duty to secure first that to which they were entitled precluded them from the prior performance of any other task. The members of the original committee who took the latter view could also urge that Mr. Redmond's original pledge that the Volunteers would "defend the shores of Ireland" was not capable of the gloss that "the shores of Ireland" under the circumstances was a legitimate figure of speech for the trenches in the front line in France. The difference of interpretation developed into a split. The members of the original committee met in September and called a Volunteer Convention for November 25, 1914, at which it was decided " to declare that Ireland cannot with honour or safety take part in foreign quarrels otherwise than through the free action of a National Government of her own; and to repudiate the claim of any man to offer up the blood and lives of the sons of Irishmen and Irishwomen to the services of the British Empire while no National Government which could act and speak for the people of Ireland is allowed to exist."

Before the split the Volunteers had numbered about 150,000; and it would appear that the great majority of these at first sided with Mr. Redmond. Many of them enlisted: many of them, under the title of the National Volunteers, continued to exist as a separate body in Ireland: some at least of them afterwards found their way back into the ranks of the Irish Volunteers.

From the time of the Volunteer split the air was cleared politically in Ireland: for the first time people began to know precisely where they stood. The National Volunteers and the Parliamentary Party under Mr. Redmond's leadership were committed, as were the Unionists, to the unreserved and energetic prosecution of the war: all the other parties, Sinn Fein, the Republicans, the Irish Volunteers, and the Citizen Army adopted an attitude of watchful neutrality. Their view was bounded by the shores of Ireland or when they cast a glance abroad it was as the husbandman observes the clouds. They continued to differ (sometimes sharply and vehemently) from one another: but the public, with a prophetic disregard of the mere obvious present, began to label them indiscriminately as Sinn Feiners. In truth common adversity was drawing them closer together, and the apparently heterogeneous elements which went to make up the Sinn Fein of present-day Ireland were being welded into a unity of aim and resolution.

The results were soon apparent. During the month or so when the Volunteers enjoyed the fleeting sunlight of aristocratic favour, the Foreign Office had written (18th August, 1914) to H.B.M. Consul-General at Antwerp to assist Mr. John O'Connor, M.P., and Mr. H. J. Harris in arranging for the shipment to Ireland of certain rifles belonging to the Volunteers, permission to export them having been obtained from the Belgian Government by the Foreign Office. It was, no doubt, an oversight that no ammunition for them was obtained, or could be obtained afterwards; but the rifles came. Three months later an officer of the Volunteers who was employed in the Ordnance Survey was dismissed without charge or notice and ordered to leave Dublin within twenty-four hours.

He was only the first of a series of Volunteer organizers who suffered deportation under similar circumstances. The Birmingham factory which was engaged in making guns for the Volunteers was raided, its books and correspondence seized, and it was ordered not to remove any goods from its premises. To be an Irish Volunteer was to be "disaffected," and to be "disaffected" was to be liable to summary measures of repression.

The autumn of 1914 saw the appearance of a new Separatist paper, *Eire-Ireland*, which appeared as a weekly on October 26th and was changed to a daily after the second number. It is significant of the change in Irish feeling that it was now possible to run a Separatist daily paper in Dublin, and of the gradual rapprochement between Irish parties that this paper, intended as the organ of the Irish Volunteers, was edited by Mr. Arthur Griffith, the founder of the Sinn Fein movement. Its attitude towards the war was defined in an article by Roger Casement in the first number: "Ireland has no quarrel with the German people or just cause of offence against them. . . . . Ireland has suffered at the hands of British administrators a more prolonged series of evils deliberately inflicted than any other community of civilized men." It emphasized the view of the Volunteers that Mr. Redmond's advice to take their place in the firing line was out of harmony with their principles. "The Irish Volunteers had from the beginning and still have but a single duty —to secure and safeguard the rights and liberties of Ireland." The new daily contained a column "The War Day by Day" in which a critical analysis of the military situation was attempted. While most of the other Irish papers merely reproduced the amateur war criticisms of Fleet Street, the editor of *Eire*, assuming that English newspapers were giving only one side of the case, attempted an independent study of the situation, which was made to appear much less favourable to the Allies than was asserted by other Irish papers. Stories of German atrocities were analyzed and ridiculed. The fortunes of the Irish regiments were followed with a jealous eye: it was asserted that they were being sacrificed unnecessarily while English regiments were spared, and the Government was challenged to prepare and publish complete casualty lists for the Irish regiments of the line. The protest of the German professors against the alleged Allied calumnies was printed in full and annotated with sympathy. The assurance given to Roger Casement by the German Acting-Secretary of State for Foreign Affairs as to the contemplated action of German troops if they should land in Ireland was printed as a document of first-rate international importance. It was assumed that the Ballot Act would be enforced in Ireland and passive resistance to its enforcement was urged from the first number of the paper. *Eire* did not run for much more than six weeks. Its last number (December 4) was a broad sheet announcing that the printer, whose premises had been entered by a military force which had confiscated his property, felt unable to continue the printing of the paper.

*Eire* did not so much make, as voice, the opinions of a considerable section of Irish Nationalist opinion. The newspapers were scanned eagerly every morning all over Ireland for tidings of the Irish regiments. It was known that they were engaged, that they were outnumbered, that they would fight like lions ("the Gaels went out to battle but they always fell"): a disquieting and ominous silence reigned as to their fate. It was assumed that the news was bad and that it was being kept back: it began to be asserted that they were being put upon forlorn hopes to spare the more valued English regiments: and even those who did not credit the suspicion felt uneasy when it was expressed. It may have been necessary to refrain from telling the whole truth in official reports, but every course has its disadvantages and, so far as Ireland was concerned, this had the result of arousing suspicion and distrust. And to the question "Why, if these men can fight and die for the freedom of others, are they not considered worthy of the freedom they desire for themselves?" the answers did not carry conviction.

The official "War News" printed in the Irish papers was read with detachment and reserve; stories of German atrocities were received with unimpressionable scepticism. This was not due to any pro-German bias, or to any Sinn Fein propaganda. Peasants in remote villages who never saw any paper but an odd copy of the *Freeman's Journal* or the *Irish Daily Independent*, and who were Redmondites to a man, discussed these matters with a completely open mind, and with (to those who did not know them) surprising acumen. People accustomed for years to read that their county or their province, in which some unpopular grazier had been boycotted, was " seething with outrage and disorder," to be told that a district in which there was known not to be as much crime in a year as there was in an English district of the same size every month was " in a state bordering on almost complete lawlessness," were not moved when the Germans were charged on the same authority with crimes against civilization. The word of " our English correspondent " was simply " not evidence" against anybody. This invincible scepticism, born of experience, was quite wrongly interpreted as being the result of " pro-German" sympathies when it proved an unexpected obstacle to the recruiting campaign.

The gradual growth of Sinn Fein and anti-English (which was only accidentally and not on principle pro-German) sentiment during the war, and the increasing difficulties found in the way of the recruiting campaign, were due mainly to a growing disbelief in the sincerity of English statesmen in their dealings with Ireland. The Government had gone too far in the direction of Home Rule to make Unionists sure that the promised Amending Bill would secure that they should not be " coerced": it had not gone far

enough to make Nationalists sure that it really
meant to do what it had promised. The result was
the conviction upon all hands that their rights
must be secured by their own efforts not by
reliance upon the lukewarm sympathy of others.
This conviction was not a matter of a sudden
growth nor did it always find expression in the
same way: it acted at once in favour of, and to the
detriment of, recruiting: it was professed both by
Nationalists and by Unionists. At first recruits
joined because the war was just, because the
Empire was in danger, because England had
granted Ireland a " charter of liberty," because
the civilization of Europe was threatened, because
there was fighting afoot. Probably the majority
enlisted for one or other of these reasons. But
the theory of "a free gift of a free people"
expounded by Mr. Asquith in Dublin fell more and
more into the background. It began to be represented on both sides that the more recruits either
party sent to the war the stronger would be the
lien of that party upon the sympathy of the English Government. Unionists whose blood had
flowed for England in Flanders could not be
abandoned after such a sacrifice: Nationalists
who had given their best and bravest to the cause
of freedom could not be denied the freedom for
which such a price had been paid. The official
recruiting campaign wavered in its appeal between
the two points. Its minor ineptitudes need hardly
be taken into account. It was hardly politic to
cover the walls of police barracks in Protestant

villages in Ulster with green placards drawing attention to a few weighty words of Cardinal Logue: these follies did neither harm nor good. But it was different when appeals to the chivalry and bravery of Irishmen alternated with deductions from the famous phrase about " the rights of small nations." When Irish Nationalists were implored to rally to the defence of the Friend of Little Nations the size of Ireland was not likely to be forgotten. The inference that in fighting for the liberties of small nations Irishmen would be helping their own nation to secure the same liberty was the inference intended: but it was not always the inference actually drawn. The person who first conceived the idea of making use of that phrase for recruiting purposes in Ireland did the cause of recruiting an unforeseen but serious disservice. Was it, after all, really true (it was asked) that England could not recognize the freedom of Ireland until Ireland had first helped England to force Germany to recognize the freedom of Belgium? Was the freedom of Ireland then not a matter of right but the result of a bargain—the equivalent of how many fighting men? Had England been the friend of small nations before the war, was she to be their friend during the war, or was Ireland only to help her to be their friend after the war was over? The right of Ireland to more freedom than she had enjoyed had seemed to be recognized before the war had been spoken of; what had become of the recognition of it? And even bargaining, however distasteful, has its usages: it was no bargain when one side was called upon to pay up and the other carefully refrained from promising anything definite in return.

The bulk of the recruits enlisted during the first year of the war, and enlisted for worthy and honourable motives: when recruiting became, as it did become later, a question of party tactics the results were less favourable. But quite early in the war it became plain that there was going to be a contest between the two Irish parties as to which should have most to show for itself at the end, and there was no burning desire to assist political opponents to obtain recruits. Sir Edward Carson refused absolutely to stand on the same recruiting platform as Mr. Redmond; the Belfast Unionist papers found it a grave lapse from principle in the present Lord Chancellor of England that he addressed a recruiting meeting in Liverpool in the company of Home Rulers. The Ulster Volunteer Force was informed practically that it had a two-fold duty, to fight for the Empire abroad, and to keep up the organization at home. It was plain from the first that in Ireland there was to be no " party truce," and it was recognized on all hands before long that when the war was over the old fight was to be renewed. The position of the Home Rule Act, penned in the Statute Book, with an Amending Bill waiting to tear it to pieces when the time came for it to be allowed out, made this inevitable. And the Government did not find it in its heart to hold an even balance between the parties: and when the balance began to dip the end was in sight for those who had eyes to see.

The only party really able to turn to account the situation thus created was the Sinn Fein party. It had preached for years that the English governing classes, indeed the English nation, were not, in spite of their apparent readiness to listen to the Parliamentary Party, the friends of Irish Nationalism in any real sense: that they had no intention (and never had) of satisfying the just claims of Ireland: that the Parliamentarians were mere pawns in a party game, to be sacrificed when it suited both or either of the English parties: that the word of English statesmen could not be trusted, and that Ireland had nothing to gain from them: that self-reliance, vigilance and distrust of England were "the sinews of good sense" in Irish politics. It had hinted, not obscurely, that the opportunity of Ireland would come when England should be involved in a European war, and that Ireland must be prepared when the day came to use the opportunity. It now pointed a triumphant finger to what was going on in Ireland and asked which had been the truer prophet, itself or the Parliamentary Party. It quoted the returns of recruiting in Ulster in support of its thesis: " The fact that out of 200,000 Unionists of military age in Ireland—men who talked Empire, sang Empire and protested they would die for the British Empire—four out of every five are still at home, declaring they will not have Home Rule, is proof that the Irish Unionist knows his present business." That Irish soldiers were to be used to further English interests, and not the cause of Ireland, was (it held) proved by extracts from English newspapers, where in unguarded moments the naked truth peeped out: it gave prominence to a quotation from the *Liverpool Post* of September 12, 1914: " His Majesty could make a triumphal tour of Ireland, North, South, East and West, and in reply to his personal appeal, there would be 300,000 Irishmen of all creeds and classes for the Front in less than a week. In England the question becomes more and more important in the interests of the efficiency of our trade, whether we can spare any more skilled mechanics for the ranks of battle. The capture of the German trade is almost as vital to the existence of the Empire as the destruction of Prussian militarism."

By the end of 1914 all avowedly Sinn Fein papers had been suppressed, and the two American papers, the *Gaelic American* and the *Irish World*, had been prohibited in Ireland. The latter had been a supporter of Mr. Redmond's policy but had parted company with him on the question of recruiting in Ireland. The editor of *Sinn Fein* countered the suppression of his paper by an ingenious device. He began to publish a bi-weekly called *Scissors and Paste*, which contained nothing but extracts from other English, Irish, Colonial and American papers. It was introduced to the reader in the only editorial it contained, entitled " Ourselves": " It is high treason," it ran, " for an

Irishman to argue with the sword the right of his small nationality to equal political freedom with Belgium or Servia or Hungary. It is destruction to the property of his printer now when he argues it with the pen. Hence while England is fighting the battle of the Small Nationalities, *Ireland* is reduced to *Scissors and Paste.* Up to the present the sale and use of these instruments have not been prohibited by the British Government in Ireland." The columns of the *Times,* the *Daily Mail,* and the *Morning Post* supplied the German Wireless messages: the *New York Times* was drawn upon for James O'Donnell Bennett's articles protesting against the reports of German atrocities. In addition it printed suitable extracts from *The Reliques of Father Prout,* from Barry's *Songs of Ireland,* Thomas Davis's *Essays* and Sir Samuel Ferguson: it reprinted Curran's speech in defence of the printer of *The Press* in 1797. It ransacked the *Daily Mail* for that journal's vigorous denunciations of the French in 1899: "If they cannot cease their insults their colonies will be taken from them and given to Germany and Italy—we ourselves want nothing more. . . . France will be rolled in the blood and mud in which her Press daily wallows." The paper ran for a little over a month. Its undoing was an extract from the *Irish Times,* a copy of a notice posted on a Sunday morning in January, 1915, in places near a number of Roman Catholic churches in Wexford: "People of Wexford, take no notice of the police order to destroy your own property and leave your own

homes if a German army lands in Ireland. When
the Germans come they will come as friends and to
put an end to English rule in Ireland. Therefore
stay in your homes and assist as far as possible the
German troops. Any stores, hay, corn or forage
taken by the Germans will be paid for by them."

Just before the disappearance of *Scissors and
Paste*, the *Irish Worker*, three weeks after its
suppression, appeared again in Glasgow, where it
was printed by the Socialist Labour Party, and
began to circulate once more in Ireland.

After five months Mr. Arthur Griffith was
again able to start a paper. The Dublin printers
could not be induced to take the risk of printing
for him again: but Belfast supplied one with
the necessary enterprise. On June 19, 1915,
*Nationality* appeared as a penny weekly paper and
continued to appear until the Easter Rising in
1916. In tone *Nationality* was a reproduction of
its predecessors and as the main characteristic of
Sinn Fein propaganda was its directness and
simplicity two extracts from its columns will
suffice. An editorial (signed C.) on " The Fenian
Faith" written towards the end of 1915 contains the
following: " The Fenians and the Fenian faith
incarnated in Allen, Larkin and O'Brien were of
a fighting and revolutionary epoch. They can
only be commemorated by men of another fighting
and revolutionary generation. That generation
we have with us to-day. For we have the material,
the men and stuff of war, the faith and purpose and
cause for revolution. . . . We shall have

Ireland illumined with a light before which even the Martyrs' will pale: the light of Freedom, of a deed done and action taken and a blow struck for the Old Land"; and a month or so later: "The things that count in Ireland against English Conscription are national determination, serviceable weapons and the knowledge of how to use them." Under the stress of circumstances Sinn Fein seemed to have abandoned the policy of the days of peace and to have come round in time of war to the policy which, even two years before the war, had been enunciated in *Irish Freedom*: "Ireland can be freed by force of arms; *that* is the fact which ever must be borne in mind. The responsibility rests with the men of this generation. They can strike with infinitely greater hopes of success than could their fathers and their grandsires: but if they let this chance slip . . . . . if they strike no blow for their country whilst England herself is in handgrips with the most powerful nation in Europe, then the opportunity will have passed and Ireland will be more utterly under the heel of England than ever she was since the Union." This was written in September, 1912. But the task of putting the policy into practice, of welding the (at times) discordant elements of anti-Parliamentarian Nationalism together and making possible a united effort was reserved for other hands and another mind than those of the founder of Sinn Fein.

During the vigorous years of its youth Sinn Fein had not confined its propagandist activities

to public meetings, the foundation of branches and
the publication of a paper. The National Council
of Sinn Fein had issued a series of "National
Council Pamphlets" dealing with those aspects of
Sinn Fein policy upon which the public seemed to
require instruction. The first of these was a
general exposition of the Sinn Fein policy by Mr.
Griffith. Others were "The Purchase of the
Railways," "England's Colossal Robbery of
Ireland," a study of the financial relations between
the two countries since the Act of Union, "Ireland
and the British Armed Forces," "Constitutionalism and Sinn Fein" and "How Ireland is
Taxed," an exposition of the fact (often ignored)
that under the Union Ireland is the most heavily
taxed country in Europe. Finally, in 1912, a
pamphlet by Mr. Griffith, "The Home Rule Bill
Examined," was a general review of the powers
conferred and withheld by the Home Rule Bill and
an examination of the real bearing of that measure
upon the political and economic situation of Ireland. The increasing difficulties which attended
the publication of a newspaper during the war, the
increased demand for information upon the situation created by it, the increasing number of those
who felt that they had something to say which
required more space than could be afforded in a
newspaper, led to a revival of the publication of
pamphlets. Early in 1915 a series of "Tracts for
the Times" was projected by the Irish Publicity
League. The first of these was a tract "What
Emmet means in 1915," significant of the direc-

tion in which minds were turning at the time. It
was followed by " Shall Ireland be Divided?" an
impassioned protest against the policy of partition
and by " The Secret History of the Irish Volunteers" (which ran through several editions), an
account by The O'Rahilly of the formation of the
Volunteers, their policy, their attempts to secure
arms and their relations with the Parliamentary
Party. The traditional Sinn Fein view was
enforced in " When the Government Publishes
Sedition," an analysis of the official census
returns, showing that under the Union the
population of Ireland had been reduced by onehalf, and in two pamphlets on " Daniel O'Connell
and Sinn Fein" an attempt was made to commend
the policy by an argument that O'Connell both in
his methods and his aims was really a Sinn
Feiner, and by an exposition (" How Ireland is
Plundered") of the question of the Financial
Relations in O'Connell's day and since. Other
pamphlets were " What it Feels Like " on the
prison experiences of the writer who had been
imprisoned under the Defence of the Realm Act
for his political activities, " Ascendancy While
You Wait" and " Why the Martyrs of Manchester
Died." During the same time the Cumann na
mBan, the women's branch of the Irish Volunteers,
added to their activities the publication of a
" National Series" of pamphlets " Why Ireland is
Poor—English Laws and Irish Industries," "Dean
Swift on the Situation" and " The Spanish War,"
a reprint of a pamphlet published in 1790 by Wolfe

Tone, urging the Irish Parliament to take into
account in the consideration of the threatened war
with Spain solely and simply the interests of
Ireland, the only interests which it should allow
itself to consider. The Committee of Public
Safety also in 1915 published a pamphlet on "The
Defence of the Realm Act in Ireland" showing
how the Act was administered for the suppression
of Nationalist propaganda. The speech which
Mr. F. Sheehy-Skeffington delivered in the dock
when charged under the same Act with interfering
with recruiting was published as a pamphlet about
the same time. The articles contributed to *Irish
Freedom* by P. H. Pearse were reprinted under the
title of "From a Hermitage" in the autumn of
1915 as one of the "Bodenstown Series" of
pamphlets, the first of which had been Mr.
Pearse's "How Does She Stand?" a reprint of
two speeches delivered in America in 1914 at
Emmet Commemorations in New York and
Brooklyn and of the eloquent speech delivered at
the grave of Wolfe Tone in Bodenstown Churchyard in 1913. The funeral of O'Donovan Rossa in
August, 1915, also produced some pamphlets on
Rossa's life and his significance as a Fenian leader
and a protagonist of the Irish Republican cause.
These pamphlets, and others, had a wide circulation; they were eagerly discussed, especially
among young Nationalists; they widened the rift
between the Parliamentary Party and their
opponents, and had much to do with the shaping
of Irish Nationalist opinion.

Meanwhile the activities of the Irish Volunteers continued. The secession after the dispute with Mr. Redmond had withdrawn a large majority of their original numbers: indeed some authorities go so far as to say that immediately after the formation of the National Volunteers, the original committee could not count upon a following of more than 10,000 or 12,000 men. Be this as it may, the arrest and deportation of several of their organizers, the constant supervision over their proceedings exercised by the police authorities and the sure drift of Nationalist opinion away from the Parliamentarians and their policy, not (it is true) so marked then as to cause serious official misgiving, tended to increase their prestige and popularity. The funds had for the most part gone with the National Volunteers, but the Irish in America, who sided not with Mr. Redmond but with the Irish Volunteers, supplied large sums of money for equipment and organization. The report of the Second Annual Convention held in November, 1915, contains a speech by the President on the history and aims of the movement which concluded: " Further I will only say that we ought all to adhere faithfully and strictly to the objects, the constitution and the policy which we have adopted. We will not be diverted from our work by tactics of provocation. We will not give way to irritation or excitement. Our business is not to make a show or indulge in demonstrations. We started out on a course of constructive work requiring a long period of patient and tenacious exertion. When things were going most easily for us, I never shrank from telling my comrades that success might require years of steady perseverance—a prospect sometimes harder to face than an enemy in the field. . . . Great progress has been made, more must be made. The one thing we must look to is that there shall be no stopping and no turning back." There were at this time over 200 corps of the Irish Volunteers in active training and the movement was spreading, if not rapidly, yet quietly and surely. The leaders waited for time to do its work, to bring fully home to Irish Nationalists the difference between a policy in which the necessities of Empire held the first place and one in which the claims of Ireland were supreme: meanwhile it was intended that the Volunteers should act as " a national defence force for Ireland, for all Ireland and for Ireland only," ready to ward off any assault upon Irish liberty, but resolved not to provoke or to invite attack.

But in spite of official policies and intentions there had slowly been formed a small but determined minority in Ireland who looked to revolution as the only sure and manly policy for a nation pledged to freedom. This, the creed of the Fenians, had not been openly avowed in Ireland for almost half a century: Nationalists had come to regard it either as a forlorn hope, a gallant but hopeless adventure, or as a policy out of harmony with modern civilization and progress. Here and there a lonely but picturesque figure might be seen, " an old Fenian," in the world but not of it,

who spoke with a resigned contempt of the new
men and the new methods, an inspiration but
hardly an example to the younger generation.
There was still in existence the Irish Republican
Brotherhood, an obscure and elusive body, mysterious as the Rosicrucians and to all outward
appearances of hardly any more political importance. A secret but apparently innocuous correspondence was understood to be kept up by them
with America where, among an important and
influential section of the expatriated Irish, the
hope was more widely and more openly cherished
of a day when Ireland would shake off the lethargy
of a generation and revert to the age-long claim for
independence. For a short time it seemed as if
the prospect of the grant of Home Rule would
quench the last embers of the revolutionary fire,
as if the English democracy had at last stretched
out a friendly hand and that the rest would be the
work of time. Ulster's appeal to arms quickened
the embers to a flame; in less than two years' time
a revolution was spoken of more openly than had
been the case for fifty years. No man in Ireland
would have taken up arms to secure Home Rule:
it was a " concession" which to some Nationalists
seemed the greatest that could be obtained, to
others (and perhaps the majority) to be a step
upon the road to a larger independence: both
sections were agreed that it should be sought by
constitutional methods. But force might be the
only means of retaining what it had been proper
to secure without it, and the Irish Volunteers were

prepared to fight those who attempted to take from the people of Ireland any right which they had been able to secure.

But it was not to be expected that the purely defensive policy of the Volunteers would commend itself to all sections of Nationalist opinion nor could the formula of their association produce more than an outward and seeming unity. So much had been true before the war; and when Europe was involved in strife, when the issue between England with her Allies and the Central Powers seemed to hang in the balance, a purely defensive and waiting policy seemed to be a criminal neglect of the opportunity offered by Providence. Mitchel's prophecy of the fortune that a continental war might bring to Ireland seemed about to be fulfilled, unless the arm of Ireland should prove nerveless and impotent. Not alone in Ireland were voices raised to point the lesson: the Irish in America who still professed the Fenian faith urged insistently the use of the opportunity. Two books written by James K. Maguire and printed by the Wolfe Tone Publishing Co. of New York, "What Could Germany do for Ireland?" and "The King, the Kaiser and Irish Freedom" had a considerable circulation in Ireland during 1915 and 1916. Written by an Irish-American who had been educated at a German school in Syracuse, and was well known for his German sympathies, they boldly announced that in a German victory lay the only hope for the establishment of an Irish Republic. They asserted not only that Germany would establish and guarantee the independence of Ireland, but that she would help Ireland to develop her industries and commerce, her resources in coal, metals and peat, which still after a hundred years of the Union were no further developed than they had been in the middle of the eighteenth century. To most Irishmen the panegyric of German disinterestedness was an idle tale, and Sinn Fein had been proclaiming (not without success) for nearly a score of years that the development of Ireland must not be expected from outsiders but from Irishmen themselves. But there were those who thought that the power to raise the heavy hand of England must be found, not in the slow efforts of a painful and hampered self-reliance, but in a hand heavier still: and it was assumed that German aid once given to free and re-establish Ireland would be withdrawn before it became tutelage and exploitation. No one dreamed of an Ireland that should exchange the penurious restraint of the Union for the prosperous servitude of a German Province: the end of all endeavour was the sovereign independence of Ireland.

The German Foreign Office, with the sanction of the Imperial Chancellor, had quite early in the war, on the motion of Roger Casement, given what was taken for an unequivocal assurance on this point. "The Imperial Government," the statement ran, "declares formally that Germany would not invade Ireland with any intentions of conquest or of the destruction of any institutions.

If, in the course of this war, which Germany did not seek, the fortunes of arms should ever bring German troops to the coast of Ireland, they would land there, not as an army of invaders coming to rob or destroy, but as the fighting forces of a Government inspired by goodwill toward a land and a people for whom Germany only wishes national prosperity and national freedom." Even a slight acquaintance with methods of imperial expansion would point to the necessity for a rigorous scrutiny of the terms of such a declaration and no such scrutiny would pronounce this declaration to be even moderately satisfactory: even if it stood the test it would not (so mysterious are the ways of State policy) have been worth the paper it was written on. But "cows over the water have long horns"—the German promise was an anchor sure and steadfast.

Whatever aid might be expected from Germany to secure the success of a revolution, nothing could be done without a party in Ireland united in its aims and able to take advantage of any aid that might be sent. No single party in Ireland could have been said to fulfil the conditions. The only Nationalist section which could have combined with an outside expeditionary force landing in Ireland was the Irish Volunteers, but not one of them was, by virtue of his Volunteer pledge, in any way bound to do so. Nor was there any guarantee that their views as to the ultimate form which a free Irish constitution should assume were identical: in fact it was known that they were not.

Official Sinn Fein still found the independence of Ireland in the Constitution of 1782: the Republicans would have nothing but a "true Republican Freedom." The Citizen Army was Republican in its teaching but it was openly hostile to both sections of the Volunteers. To it Sinn Fein and many of the Republicans seemed a bourgeois party, from which the workers need expect nothing. To James Connolly, their leader, the vaunted prosperity reached under the independent Irish Parliament was the prosperity of a class and not of the community, and he could point to the writings of Arthur O'Connor, ignored by orthodox Sinn Feiners, in proof of his contention. To establish the political ideals of Sinn Fein the Citizen Army was not prepared to raise its little finger. The Republicans might have seemed more sympathetic and congenial allies; but many even of them seemed too remote and formal in their ideals, too much wrapped up in visions of a future Ireland, free and indivisible, to have time to spare for the formulation of the means by which all Irishmen might really be free. But there were not wanting men on both sides who saw the necessity of union in the face of a common danger for the furtherance of a common purpose, who taught that if Labour should pledge itself to Ireland, Ireland should also pledge itself to Labour. This union when it came about was mainly due to James Connolly and P. H. Pearse.

James Connolly had been for several years the acknowledged leader of Irish Socialism. His book on *Labour in Irish History* written in 1910 is recognized as a standard work: his *Reconquest of Ireland*, his pamphlet *The New Evangel*, and his articles in *The Irish Worker* were widely read and had great influence among Irish Nationalists who belonged to the Labour movement. His attitude to the two main Irish parties was one of hostility: he was hostile to the Unionists as representing the party of tyranny and privilege, to the Home Rulers as the followers of a policy which was "but a cloak for the designs of the middle-class desirous of making terms with the Imperial Government it pretends to dislike." To ardent and vague talk about "Ireland" and "freedom" he opposed the cool and critical temper of one who was accustomed to look stern facts in the face: "Ireland as distinct from her people," he wrote, "is nothing to me; and the man who is bubbling over with love and enthusiasm for 'Ireland,' and can yet pass unmoved through our streets and witness all the wrong and the suffering, the shame and the degradation brought upon the people of Ireland—aye, brought by Irishmen upon Irish men and women—without burning to end it, is in my opinion a fraud and a liar in his heart, no matter how he loves that combination of chemical elements he is pleased to call 'Ireland'." Connolly believed in Irish Nationality, but he would not have been satisfied with the right to wear the badges of independence; a national flag, a national parliament, a national culture were in themselves nothing; but if they meant the right of the common men and women of

Ireland to control their own lives and their own destinies then they meant everything in the world to him. Like Wolfe Tone he believed in " that numerous and respectable class, the men of no property"; to secure their rights in Ireland he was ready for anything. The national mould in which his Socialism came to be cast did not always appeal to his followers and associates: they regretted his increasing devotion to Irish Nationalism and his apparent indifference to pure Socialism; as one said later, " The high creed of Irish Nationalism became his daily rosary, while the higher creed of international humanity that had so long bubbled from his eloquent lips was silent for ever." As a matter of fact he tested alike theoretical Nationalism and theoretical Socialism by the facts; Nationalism, to be worth anything, must secure the rights of the common men and women who make up the bulk of the nation: Socialism, to be worth anything, must secure the rights not of " humanity" but of the human beings which compose it, and the principal human beings whose destiny an Irish Socialist could influence were the Irish. Connolly had never shared the extreme hostility to the Irish Volunteers which was characteristic of the bulk of the Citizen Army: while he championed the rights of his class he recognized that they formed, along with others, an Irish nation and that their surest charter of freedom would be the charter of freedom of their country. But it must be a real, universal and effective freedom if it were to be worth the winning. Under his guidance and influence the ideals of the Citizen Army began to approximate more closely to those of the Irish Volunteers.

The Irish Volunteers on the other hand were learning under other guidance to examine more closely the implications of the phrase "the independence of Ireland." Their guide was P. H. Pearse, a man of great gifts, a high and austere spirit filled with a great purpose. Through all his work, both in English and in Irish, plays, poems and stories, runs the thread of an ardent devotion to goodness and beauty, to spiritual freedom, to the faith that tries to move mountains and is crushed beneath them. For many years his life seems to have been passed in the grave shadow of the sacrifice he felt that he was called upon to make for Ireland: he believed that he was appointed to tread the path that Robert Emmet and Wolfe Tone had trodden before him, and his life was shaped so that it might be worthy of its end.

To Pearse the ideal Irishman was Wolfe Tone, and it is significant that one of the first occasions upon which the Irish Volunteers and the Citizen Army held a joint demonstration was a pilgrimage to Tone's grave at Bodenstown. It was here that Pearse in 1913 delivered an eloquent and memorable address in which he proclaimed his belief that Wolfe Tone was the greatest Irishman who had ever lived. "We have come," his speech began, "to the holiest place in Ireland; holier to us even than the place where Patrick sleeps in Down. Patrick brought us life, but this man died for us."

Pearse saw in Tone the greatest of all Irishmen because he saw in him the most complete incarnation of the Irish race, of its passion for freedom, its gallantry, its essential tolerance: and he urged his hearers not to let Tone's work and example perish. Quoting Tone's famous declaration of his objects and his means, of breaking the connection with England by uniting the whole people of Ireland, Pearse concluded: " I find here implicit all the philosophy of Irish Nationalism, all the teaching of the Gaelic League, and the later prophets. Ireland one and Ireland free—is not this the definition of Ireland a Nation? To that definition and to that programme we declare our adhesion anew; pledging ourselves as Tone pledged himself—and in this sacred place, by this graveside, let us not pledge ourselves unless we mean to keep our pledge—we pledge ourselves to follow in the steps of Tone, never to rest, either by day or by night, until his work be accomplished, deeming it to be the proudest of all privileges to fight for freedom, to fight not in despondency but in great joy, hoping for the victory in our day, but fighting on whether victory seem near or far, never lowering our ideal, never bartering one jot or tittle of our birthright, holding faith to the memory and the inspiration of Tone, and accounting ourselves base as long as we endure the evil thing against which he testified with his blood."

To show that Wolfe Tone was a revolutionary, that he aimed at the complete overthrow of English ascendancy in Ireland and at the severing of all political connection between the two countries, that he believed in an Ireland in which the designations of Catholic and Protestant should be swallowed up in the common bonds of nationhood —all this needed no proving, for it was matter of common knowledge with all to whom Tone's name was known. But it was necessary to do more than this. Pearse had to show in the first place that Tone might be taken as the normal and classical representative of the Irish national ideal, and in the second place that he was no mere ordinary constitution-monger but a teacher of a philosophy of nationality, valid not for his own age only, but always, capable of furnishing guidance in the just and orderly upbuilding of a modern community, of satisfying at once the claims of the nation and the claims of its humblest member. To this task he gave the last months of his life: the last four " Tracts for the Times" were from his pen: the first was written at the end of 1915, the last in March, 1916, a fortnight before the Rising. The first of these four pamphlets was entitled "Ghosts," a title borrowed from Ibsen. It is an exposition of the national teaching of five Irish leaders, Wolfe Tone, Thomas Davis, James Fintan Lalor, John Mitchel and Charles Stewart Parnell, all of whom held and taught that the national claim of Ireland was for independence and separation; their ghosts haunt the generation which has disowned them, they will not be appeased till their authority is again acknowledged. A few sentences will make the thesis of this tract (and to some extent of the following tracts) clear. "There has been nothing more terrible in Irish history than the failure of the last generation. Other generations have failed in Ireland, but they have failed nobly; or, failing ignobly, some man among them has redeemed them from infamy by the splendour of his protest. But the failure of the last generation has been mean and shameful, and no man has arisen from it to do a splendid thing in virtue of which it shall be forgiven. The whole episode is squalid. It will remain the one sickening chapter in a story which, gallant or sorrowful, has everywhere else some exaltation of pride. . . . . Even had the men themselves been less base, their failure would have been inevitable. When one thinks over the matter for a little one sees that they have built upon an untruth. They have conceived of nationality as a material thing whereas it is a spiritual thing. . . . . Hence, the nation to them is not all holy, a thing inviolate and inviolable, a thing that a man dare not sell or dishonour on pain of eternal perdition. They have thought of nationality as a thing to be negotiated about as men negotiate about a tariff or about a trade route. . . . I make the contention that the national demand of Ireland is fixed and determined; that that demand has been made by every generation; that we of this generation receive it as a trust from our fathers; that we are bound by it; that we have not the right to alter it or to abate it by one jot or tittle; and that any undertaking made in the name of Ireland to accept in full satisfaction of Ireland's claim anything less than the generations of Ireland have stood for is null and void. . . . . The man who in the name of Ireland accepts as a " final settlement " anything less by one fraction of an iota than separation from England will be repudiated by the new generation as surely as O'Connell was repudiated by the generation that came after him. The man who in return for the promise of a thing which is not merely less than separation but which denies separation and declares the Union perpetual, the man who in return for this declares peace between England and Ireland and sacrifices to England as a peace-holocaust the blood of 50,000 Irishmen is guilty of so immense an infidelity, so immense a crime against the Irish nation, that one can only say of him that it were better for that man (as it were certainly better for his country) that he had not been born." The pamphlet concludes with a historic retrospect of the Irish struggle for independence till the end of the seventeenth century, of the Anglo-Irish claim for independence in the eighteenth century, and with quotations from the five great Irish leaders since the last decade of that century joining in the same claim.

The next tract, " The Separatist Idea," was a detailed study of Wolfe Tone's political teaching. Tone was not merely a " heroic soul," he possessed an " austere and piercing intellect," which, " dominating Irish political thought for over a century," had given Ireland " its political definitions and values." Tone had written in his *Autobiography*, " I made speedily [in 1790] what was to me a great discovery, though I might have found it in Swift or Molyneux, that the influence of England was the radical vice of our Government, and that consequently Ireland would never be either free, prosperous or happy until she was independent and that independence was unattainable whilst the connection with England existed." In a pamphlet called " An Argument on behalf of the Catholics of Ireland" Tone (signing himself " A Northern Whig") had tried to convince the Dissenters " that they and the Catholics had but one common interest and one common enemy: that the depression and slavery of Ireland was produced and perpetuated by the divisions existing between them, and that, consequently, to assert the independence of their country, and their own individual liberties, it was necessary to forget all former feuds, to consolidate the entire strength of the whole nation and to form for the future but one people." In his earlier years Tone had not been a Republican, but Republicanism was the creed which he finally professed. He defined the aim of of an Irish Constitution as the promotion of " The Rights of Man in Ireland." To secure this end reliance must be had not on a section of the nation but on the nation as a whole. " If the men of property will not support us," he said, " they must fall: we can support ourselves by the aid of that numerous and respectable class of the community —the men of no property." " In this glorious appeal to Cæsar," comments Pearse, " modern Irish democracy has its origin." Tone then was not merely a Republican and a Separatist but a Democrat prepared for a democratic and revolutionary policy.

In his next tract " The Spiritual Nation" Pearse analyzed the national teaching of Thomas Davis, who was to him the embodiment of the idea of the spiritual side of nationality. Davis was a Separatist (Pearse puts this, by quotation from his writings, beyond reasonable doubt) but he laid stress more upon the spiritual than upon the material side of Irish independence. He saw in nationality " the sum of the facts, spiritual and intellectual, which mark off one nation from another," the language, the folklore, the literature, the music, the art, the social customs. "The insistence on the spiritual fact of nationality is Davis's distinctive contribution to political thought in Ireland, but it is not the whole of Davis." To secure spiritual independence, material freedom is necessary, and such freedom can only be found in political independence. One rhetorical paragraph of Davis's makes his attitude clear. " Now, Englishmen, listen to us. Though you were to-morrow to give us the best tenures on earth—though you were to equalise Presbyterian, Catholic and Episcopalian—though you were to give us the amplest representation in your Senate —though you were to restore our absentees, disencumber us of your debt, and redress every one of our fiscal wrongs—and though, in addition to all this, you plundered the treasuries of the world to lay gold at our feet and exhausted the resources of your genius to do us worship and honour—still we tell you—we tell you in the name of liberty and country—we tell you in the name of enthusiastic hearts, thoughtful souls and fearless spirits— we tell you by the past, the present and the future, we would spurn your gifts if the condition were that Ireland should remain a province. We tell you and all whom it may concern, come what may —bribery or deceit, justice, policy or war—we tell you, in the name of Ireland, that Ireland shall be a nation."

In the last pamphlet, "The Sovereign People," Pearse essayed the hardest task of all. It was introduced by the short preface, dated 31st March, 1916, "This pamphlet concludes the examination of the Irish definition of freedom which I promised in ' Ghosts.' For my part I have no more to say." It is told that he entreated the printer to have it published at once: he wished his last words, the final manifesto of his party, to be in the hands of the public before he went into the Rising. The tract is an attempt to establish, on the basis of the writings of James Fintan Lalor, the thesis that the independence claimed for Ireland is of a republican and democratic type. He expressed his views clearly and unequivocally upon such questions as the rights of private property, the individual ownership of the material resources of the community, and universal suffrage. Pearse's views as expressed in this pamphlet are seen to be practically identical with those of James Connolly, and there is little doubt that it was upon the basis of some such understanding that Pearse's followers and those of Connolly joined forces at the last. "The nation's sovereignty," the exposition runs, "extends not only to all the men and women of the nation, but to all the material possessions of the nation, the nation's soil and all its resources, all wealth and all wealth-producing processes within the nation. In other words, no private right to property is good as against the public right of the nation. But the nation is under a moral obligation so to exercise its public right as to secure strictly equal rights and liberties to every man and woman within the nation. . . . . No class in the nation has rights inferior to those of any other class. No class in the nation is entitled to privileges superior to those of any other class. . . . . To insist upon the sovereign control of the nation over all the property within the nation is not to disallow the right to private property. It is for the nation to determine to what extent private property may be held by its members and in what items of the nation's material resources private property may be allowed. A nation may, for instance, determine, as the free Irish nation determined and enforced for many centuries, that private ownership shall not exist in land, that the whole of a nation's soil is the public property of the nation. . . . . There is nothing divine or sacrosanct in any of these arrangements; they are matters of purely human concern, matters for discussion and adjustment between the members of a nation, matters to be decided on finally by the nation as a whole; and matters in which the nation as a whole can revise or reverse its decision whenever it seems good in the common interests to do so. . . . . In order that the people may be able to choose as a legislation and as a government men and women really and fully representative of themselves, they will keep the choice actually or virtually in the hands of the whole people . . . they will, if wise, adopt the widest possible franchise—give a vote to every adult man and woman of sound mind. To restrict the franchise in any respect is to prepare the way for some future usurpation of the rights of the sovereign people. The people, that is the whole people, must remain sovereign not only in theory but in fact. . . . . It is in fact true that the repositories of the Irish tradition, as well the spiritual tradition of nationality as the kindred tradition of stubborn physical resistance to England, have been the great, faithful, splendid, common people, that dumb multitudinous throng which sorrowed during the penal night, which bled in '98, which starved in the Famine; and which is here still— what is left of it—unbought and unterrified. Let no man be mistaken as to who will be lord in Ireland, when Ireland is free. The people will be lord and master." These theses are enforced by quotations from Lalor, the most outspoken Democrat and Radical in the tradition of Irish nationalism. The pamphlet concludes with a defence of John Mitchel (who adopted Lalor's teaching) against the charge of hating the English people. "Mitchel, the least apologetic of men, was at pains to explain that his hate was not of English men and women, but of the English thing which called itself a government in Ireland, of the English Empire, of English commercialism supported by English militarism, a thing wholly evil, perhaps the most evil thing that there has ever been in the world."

On Palm Sunday, 1916, the Union of Irish Labour and Irish Nationality was proclaimed in a striking fashion. In the evening of that day Connolly hoisted over Liberty Hall, the headquarters of the Citizen Army, the Irish tricolour of orange, white and green, the flag designed by the Young Irelanders in 1848 to symbolise the union of the Orange and Green by the white bond of a common brotherhood. On Easter Monday the Irish Republic was proclaimed in arms in Dublin.

## AFTER THE RISING.

There are many interesting topics of enquiry in connection with the Easter Rising: but they relate to points of detail or affect the responsibility of individuals; they do not concern the history of Sinn Fein. The Rising was the work not of Sinn Fein, but of the leaders of the Republican Party in the Irish Volunteers and of the Citizen Army. Of the signatories to the proclamation of the Republic only one had any sort of connection with Sinn Fein and he had been a reforming, rather than an orthodox, Sinn Feiner. But the general public, some from mere instinct, others from a desire to discredit a movement which they disliked and feared, persisted in calling the Rising by the name of the " Sinn Fein Rebellion," and substituted " Sinn Fein" for " Irish" in speaking of the Volunteers. In truth it would have been impossible for Sinn Fein, even if it had wished to do so, to repudiate all responsibility for the Rising. It had from the beginning proclaimed the independence of Ireland, not (it is true) in the form of an Irish Republic, but in the form of a National Constitution free from any subordination to the Parliament of England: it had renounced the idea of an appeal to arms in view of the certain failure of an armed rising: but it had not repudiated revolution upon principle and it had admitted that in certain contingencies Ireland might with propriety appeal to arms to secure its independence. The only criticism it could make upon the Rising would have been that it was a well-intentioned error of judgment, the error of men who had mistaken their means and their opportunity for accomplishing an object good in itself. It is highly improbable that any such criticism would under the circumstances have been made in public by the leaders of Sinn Fein : in any case they were not afforded the opportunity to make it, for they were arrested and deported as part of the measures of repression taken after the Rising had collapsed.

At the time of the Rising Ireland was still far from being either Sinn Fein or Republican. The prestige of parliamentarianism had been shaken and its strength impaired : expectations had been disappointed, but the reasons for the failure were still the subject of keen discussion, and the Sinn Fein explanation was by no means universally accepted. Convinced Republicans were a minority, insignificant except for their ability and fervour. The mass of Nationalists felt disturbed and uneasy. It was plain that their cause was losing ground, and that mere pre-occupation with the war was not the sole reason for the growing indifference of England to the government of Ireland. Nationalist Ireland was represented (by people who affected to speak more in sorrow than in anger) as having disowned the patriotic lead of Mr. Redmond and as failing in its duty, and this view was clearly becoming the prevalent view in England. The policy pursued by the War Office towards Nationalist recruits (a policy described by a member of the War Cabinet as "malignant") was slowly killing recruiting, and the decline of recruiting was claimed to be a justification of the policy that produced it, and that by people perfectly well aware of the facts. The favour shown to the Ulster Volunteers had not induced them to go in a body to the war: but while they were reported to have done magnificently, the National Volunteers were held to have done little and to have done it with a bad grace. The advent of the Coalition Government, which included some of the bitterest enemies of Irish Nationalism, did not mend matters. Mr. Redmond, it is true, was offered a seat in the Coalition Cabinet and declined the offer. It seemed to many Irishmen at the time that Mr. Redmond might very well have accepted it: that having stretched a point in promising Irish assistance in the war out of gratitude for a coming recognition of Irish claims, it was a mere standing upon ceremony to refuse to stretch another point and enter an English Ministry. But Mr. Redmond decided in view of the state of feeling in Ireland that he had gone as far as was prudent. His generous enthusiasm had received a shock, first in the hints of Irish disapproval at his failure to take full advantage of his opportunity, secondly when he came into contact with the cold hostility of the War Office. His slowly waning influence in Ireland might have vanished if he had advanced farther on the path of unconditional co-operation.

It had been for years a maxim—the maxim—of the Nationalist Party to accept no office under the Union Constitution, and no office under the Crown until the claims of Ireland had been conceded. These claims had not been conceded, and the prospect that they would ever be conceded was growing fainter. Had he represented Ireland under an Irish Constitution, even a Provisional Constitution, the case would have been different: Nationalist Ireland would have followed him, as England then followed Mr. Asquith: but to enter the Cabinet under the circumstances as the representative of Ireland seemed to be merely to forfeit by his entry the only ground upon which he had a claim to enter it. His decision left the way open to the almost unfettered activities of the opponents of his policy both in England and in Ireland. The strength of England in time of war, the readiness of her public men to subordinate, within limits, the strife of parties to the interests of the Commonwealth, meant the weakness of Ireland in the end. It was loudly proclaimed in England that the happy co-operation of days of stress must not be allowed to be broken up when peace dawned: that the strife of parties must be mitigated when war was over: but Ireland knew that she had been in later years their chief battleground, and that any mitigation of their quarrel, while it might be to the advantage of English public life, could only be brought about at the expense of her national hopes. And in Ireland the Executive, pursuing a fixed anti-national policy, tempered only by the prudence, the theoretical liberalism, or the bland indifference of successive Chief Secretaries, could henceforth count on the steady backing of friends in power over the water.

The Rising came like a flash of lightning in an evening twilight, illuminating and terrifying. It was not entirely unexpected: those whose duty and those whose pleasure it is to suspect everything had been uneasy for some time. The few people who were in touch with the inner circles of the Irish Volunteers had long known that something was in progress. But the authorities had nothing definite to go upon, and the majority of Irishmen knew nothing definite about it. When news came that Dublin had been seized, that an Irish Republic had been proclaimed, and that troops were hurrying across from England, the prevailing feeling was one of stupefaction. Even the Unionist newspapers, never at a loss before in pointing the Irish moral, were stunned for the moment. When the facts began to be realized, Unionist and Nationalist joined in a common condemnation of the Rising, which, unable to accomplish its professed aim, could have no real effect beyond that of hampering the Allied cause. Later on Nationalists began to fear and Unionists to hope that it meant the death of Home Rule, or at least its postponement to an indefinite future.

When the Rising was crushed and the leaders and their followers had surrendered it is questionable whether the fortunes of Republicanism in Ireland had ever been at so low an ebb. All their plans had miscarried; their very counsels had been contradictory and confused. German assistance had disappointed them; the country had not supported them; and the army had made an end of their resistance and had brought their strongholds about their heads: their leaders were in custody, not even as prisoners of war: all of their followers who had shown that they could be counted on were either dead or in gaol. There was no district in Ireland that had not sent men to the war: many of them had died at the hands of the Germans to whom the Republican leaders had looked for aid, many of them were risking their lives every hour; it was not from the friends and neighbours of these men that sympathy for the Rising could have been expected. Sinn Fein was involved in the general feeling; if it had not fomented the Rising, what had it done to discourage it? Was it not the stimulus which had spurred more daring spirits into action?

A bruised reed never seemed less difficult to break or less worth the breaking. It was decided to break it *ad majorem cautelam*.

Four days after the surrender Pearse and two others after a secret trial were shot in the morning: the next day and the next others were shot. There was a pause of three days, and the shooting was resumed till thirteen had paid the penalty. After the thirteenth execution, a proclamation was issued that the General Officer Commanding in Chief had "found it imperative" to inflict these punishments, which it was hoped would act as a

## AFTER THE RISING

deterrent and show that such proceedings as those of the Rising could not be tolerated. Two more executions followed, that of James Connolly and another. At the same time arrests took place all over the country. Three thousand prisoners who had taken no part in the Rising were collected, many of them as innocent of any complicity in the affair as the Prime Minister. To have been at any time a member of the Irish Volunteers was sufficient cause for arrest and deportation. They were taken through the streets in lorries and in furniture vans at the dead of night and shipped for unknown destinations.

In a normally governed country, a strong Government enjoying the support of the community has a comparatively easy task in dealing with an unsuccessful rebellion, if a rebellion should occur. It can shoot the leaders, if it thinks them worth shooting, or do practically what it pleases with them, and gain nothing but credit for its firmness or clemency (as the case may be). But in a country not normally governed (and no one either inside or outside Ireland considered the Irish government to be normal) the matter is more intricate. If the Government is united, has clean hands and unlimited force, and is prepared to employ force indefinitely, it may do as it pleases: but few Governments are in this position and those which are not have to pick their steps. In the case of the Easter Rising the Government began by going forward with great confidence beyond the point whence retreat was possible and then deter-

mined very carefully to pick its steps back again.
At first it acted "with vigour and firmness": it
handed the situation over to the care of a competent and tried officer, who proceeded to treat it
as a mere matter of departmental routine. He was
alert, prompt and businesslike. He did not
hesitate to take what seemed "necessary steps"
or to speak out where speaking plainly seemed
called for. He let it be known that he had come
to act and he did what he had come for.

During the week of the executions an almost
unbroken silence reigned in Ireland. The first
hint that anything was wrong came on the cables
from America. The men who were shot in Dublin
had been accorded a public funeral in New York.
Empty hearses followed by a throng of mourners
had passed through streets crowded with sympathisers standing with bared heads. Anxious
messages from British agents warned the Government that a demonstration like this could not be
disregarded. The executions were over, but the
Prime Minister decided to go to Ireland to enquire
into the situation on the spot. When he landed
the tide of Irish feeling had already turned.

The catastrophic change of feeling in Ireland is
not difficult to explain. The Rising had occurred
suddenly and had ended in a sudden and hopeless
failure. The leaders and their followers had surrendered, and the authorities held them at their
absolute disposal. The utter hopelessness of any
attempt to establish a Republic, or effect any other
change in the government of Ireland by armed

force, especially at such a time, had been clearly demonstrated. England held Ireland in the hollow of its hand. After four days' cool deliberation it was decided to shoot the leaders. They were not brought to open trial on the charge of high treason or on any other charge: the authorities who carried out the sentence were those who passed judgment upon their guilt and the only people who ever heard or saw the evidence upon which the judgment was based. They were shot in batches: for days the lesson was hammered home in stroke after stroke that these men were entitled neither to open trial and proof of their guilt before execution, nor to the treatment of captured enemies. The conclusion drawn by Nationalist Ireland was that if they had been Englishmen they would have been tried by English courts and sentenced by the judgment of their countrymen: that if they had been Germans or Turks they would have been treated as prisoners of war: but that being Irishmen they were in a class apart, members of a subject race, the mere property of a courtmartial. The applause of Parliament when the Prime Minister announced the executions was taken to represent the official sanction of the English people and their agreement with this attitude towards Ireland. It was resented in Ireland with a fierce and sudden passion: a tongue of flame seemed to devour the work of long years in a single night. After the execution of Pearse it would have been vain to argue against him that he had appealed to Germany for aid and invited

to Ireland hands red with the blood of Irish
soldiers: the reply would have been that he might
have done so or he might not; that it had never
been proved what he did; that he had acted for the
best; that

> What matters it, if he was Ireland's friend?
> There are but two great parties in the end.

The Prime Minister, less than a month after the
Rising, spent a week in Ireland prosecuting
enquiries: they resulted in two conclusions, one
that " the existing machinery of Irish government" had broken down, the other that a unique
opportunity had offered itself for a settlement.
Negotiations for the desired settlement were, on
the Prime Minister's invitation, begun by Mr.
Lloyd George. He contented himself with taking
up the first settlement that came to hand, the old
proposal for partition; but during the negotiations he left the idea in the mind of the Nationalist
leader that the partition proposed was only temporary and in the mind of the Unionist leader that
it was to be permanent. Each asserted that Mr.
Lloyd George had been explicit in his statement,
and the unexplained discrepancy wrecked the
negotiations. Even had they succeeded between
the parties principally concerned, they would
never have led to anything; for the Unionist
members of the Coalition when there seemed to
be a risk of agreement, declared that they would
have no settlement at all. The Prime Minister

and his deputy yielded and reconstituted "the
existing machinery of Irish government" by re-
appointing the former Viceroy and replacing the
Liberal Chief Secretary by a Unionist. Apparently
their chief object was not so much to make the
Government in Ireland acceptable to Irishmen as
to make it less objectionable to Unionists. The
result in Ireland was what might have been foreseen. Any idea there may have been that the
English Government was really desirous of establishing peace and justice in Ireland vanished like
smoke. Mr. Redmond warned the Government of
the consequences of their "inaction" (if any
policy which was steadily producing the most profound revulsion in Irish feeling could be described
by that word) but the Government was obdurate.
It refused to release the interned suspects, it
refused to treat them as political prisoners, it
refused to mitigate the application of martial law:
and gave as its reason the fact that the state of
the country still "gave cause for anxiety." The
only party that had no cause for "anxiety" as to
its future was Sinn Fein.

The resentment at the execution of the leaders
of the Rising had not confined itself to the indul-
gence of feelings of rage and sorrow. It had led
to an eager inquiry into what it was that had
caused these men to do what they did. People
who had hardly heard of Sinn Fein before wanted
to know precisely what it was and what it taught:
people who had not known Pearse and Connolly
when they were alive were full of curiosity about

them, their principles and their writings. Much
of this curiosity was morbid and led nowhere: but
a great deal of it led large numbers of people very
far indeed. Sinn Fein pamphlets began to be in
demand: a month after the Rising it was hardly
possible to procure a single one of them. But if
they could not be bought, thumbed and tattered
copies were passed from hand to hand: their teachings and the doctrines of Sinn Fein were discussed
all over Ireland. The (to many) surprising fact
became known that the Rising was not an attempt
to help Germany or to put Ireland into German
possession, but to free Ireland from all foreign
influence: that the leaders proclaimed themselves
followers of Tone and Mitchel and Davis and
Parnell, that they claimed that Irish Nationalism
meant according to these exponents (and no man
in Ireland ventured to question their authority)
Irish independence, nothing less and nothing
more. The instinct for freedom, the feeling that
the existing Government of Ireland had not for
a hundred years fulfilled the primary functions of
government, became a reasoned and rooted conviction that something more was needed to mend
it than mere Home Rule. The price that Ireland
had been asked to pay for Home Rule, that it was
still pertinaciously pressed to agree to, the partition of Ireland, seemed an unforgivable treachery
beside the fair prospect of an Ireland one and
indivisible, in which Orange and Green, Protestant
and Catholic were united in the love and service
of a common country. The policies of the past,

barren as they now seemed of content and substance, were abandoned for the new promise of a commonwealth in which all Irishmen should be equal, in which the worker saw a prospect of a better and a fuller life than without it he could hope to have. This had been the ideal of the Rising; but it was the bitter truth that the Rising had not brought it any nearer, and that no Rising seemed likely to be any more successful. Sinn Fein with its policy of self-reliance, of refusing to recognize what it hoped by so doing to bring to nothing, of distrust of all policies of reaching freedom by an acknowledgment of subjection offered the means of realizing what the Rising had failed to bring nearer. But Sinn Fein could not be accepted as it stood: offering the Constitution of 1782 it had failed to carry with it more than a few doctrinaire enthusiasts: agreeing to the constitution which the leaders of the Rising died for it might (and did) carry the country with it.

All this was going on under the operation of martial law. Members of Parliament did not know it: the Competent Military Authority had no suspicion of it. It was believed that all that was required to "appease" the country, to restore confidence in the Government, to bring back the happy days when Ireland was "the one bright spot" was to release the prisoners and resume negotiations for a "settlement." In December, 1916, the Asquith Ministry fell. According to its successors it had carried the art of doing nothing to its highest perfection: they were going to do everything at once. The new Prime Minister made vague promises of an attempt to settle the Irish question in the immediate future, and finally on Christmas Eve all the interned prisoners except those undergoing penal servitude, were sent back to Ireland. They were received with an enthusiasm which must have proved disquieting to the believers in compromise and negotiation.

Everything began again precisely where it had left off. The prisoners had been requested to give a pledge that, if released, they would cease to engage in political propaganda objectionable to the Government. This they had stoutly refused to do, and they had been released at last without conditions. Apparently it was supposed that the operation of martial law and the promises of the new Government would exercise a moderating influence: but martial law was only a standing challenge, and the sincerity of the Government was no longer believed in. If it had been even moderately sincere it might have rallied to the side of compromise those large numbers of men who in every country have an instinctive dread of new and untried policies and leaders. But it was soon plain that a Prime Minister pledged to everybody was pledged to nobody.

By the middle of February, 1917, the Sinn Fein leaders were at work again. *Nationality* reappeared as a weekly paper. It appealed no longer to a few enthusiasts but to a wide public eager to learn more of the only movement which promised anything definite. Before the Rising Sinn Fein

had seemed to aim at the impossible by means
beyond the powers of average human nature: it
did not seem possible that any large body of Irishmen should try to secure independence by the hard
path of Sinn Fein, when there was a prospect of
something (to all outward appearance) nearly as
good to be gained by recording a vote for the right
man at elections. It was now plain to the average
Nationalist that the parliamentary prospect held
no promise: that the Irish Parliamentary Party
were no longer listened to, and that the sworn
enemies of Irish nationality were in the seats of
power both in Ireland and in England. Mr.
Redmond, confronted alternately in England by
the iron insolence of the Tories and the smiling
sinuosities of the Prime Minister, manned his guns
to the last: but he had no longer the support of the
country. The country was beginning to rally to
the party which alone seemed to be the party of
fixed principles: which had another standard by
which to measure national rights than the temporary possibilities, varying from month to month,
offered by the difficulties confronting English
Ministers: the party which did not entreat but
demanded. Sinn Fein did not promise now any
more than in the days of its obscurity that national
freedom could be won by the anaemic struggles of
the division lobbies in the House: it warned its
followers that the way would be long and steep,
that to shun the steep places was to miss the track,
and that the path did not cross the water. It had
said this before, but it said it now to ears ready

to receive it. If men had died for Ireland (men asked) facing the old enemy, what lesser sacrifice could be called too great? A wave of enthusiasm which no appeal to policy or prudence could withstand swept over the country when the new campaign began.

*Nationality* with a tenacity of purpose that nothing seemed able to disturb began its new series with the old lesson, the decay of Ireland under the Union. As if there had been no Rising, no imprisonments, no threats of summary repression, the doctrine was again proclaimed with deadly deliberation that the Union had destroyed and was destroying the prosperity of Ireland even in those districts which clung to it with most affection. The population of Antrim, Armagh, Derry and Down was steadily declining under a system which the inhabitants declared essential to their continued existence. It asserted the right of Ireland to prevent food being exported from the country to feed strangers while the country that supplied it was left to starve, and proposed the formation of a Watch Committee for every seaport in the country. The very first number contained a statement of the policy of an appeal no longer to a Government pledged to disregard it, but to the Peace Conference which must be summoned on the conclusion of the war. The advertisement of the Irish Nation League, a body independent of Sinn Fein, already showed how far Sinn Fein principles had spread in Ireland. " The Irish Nation League claims the right of Ireland to recognition as a Sovereign State. It asserts too and claims Ireland's right to representation at any International Peace Conference. It offers determined and resolute resistance to any attempt to enforce Conscription. . . . It calls on the Irish people to rely on themselves alone. . . . . . Members elected under the auspices of the Irish Nation League will remain under the control of its Supreme Council and will only act at Westminster when the Council so decides. Never again must power be placed in the hands of a parliamentary party to mislead the country or to sacrifice opportunities." In March *Nationality* announced the formation of a National Council to support the admission of Ireland to the Peace Conference and " to safeguard the general interests of the nation." But though admission to the Peace Conference was the political objective of Ireland for the moment it was not regarded as its ultimate or only aim. The Peace Conference was an opportunity to be made use of when circumstances brought it about, a precious and unique opportunity, but Ireland's main and serious work was to develop her own resources and her own powers of resistance. Accordingly, though Sinn Fein declared repeatedly its intention of carrying the Irish case before the Peace Conference, its main work was still to organize and consolidate opposition to the two chief measures now openly proclaimed as in contemplation, the partition of Ireland and the enforcement of Conscription. Both these measures were in contradiction to the claim that " the only satisfactory settlement of the Irish Question now is the independence of Ireland." And it was not hard to show that the professed objects of the war were incompatible with the policy of refusing self-government to Ireland. "When England declared," wrote *Nationality*, "that she entered this war with the object of asserting the freedom of Small Nations the Lord delivered her into our hands."

There were not wanting signs that the Sinn Fein policy was rapidly becoming the policy of a Nationalist Ireland. By the summer of 1917 at least a dozen Irish newspapers were declared exponents of the Sinn Fein policy. An election for North Roscommon in February had resulted in the return of the Sinn Fein candidate by an overwhelming majority. The next contested election was in May and was by common consent regarded as a test election. It was a straight fight between the Parliamentary Party and Sinn Fein. Each party put its full strength into the contest and Sinn Fein won; the majority, it is true, was a small one but it was more useful than a large one, for it was both an endorsement and an incentive. The *Manchester Guardian* frankly declared that the Sinn Fein victory under the circumstances was equivalent to a serious defeat of the British Army in the field.

The reply of the Government to the result of the North Roscommon election had been the re-arrest and deportation of some of the released prisoners, to whom a number of others, some of them prominent Gaelic Leaguers, were added; the Chief Secretary defended this action by saying that he had decided " although there can be no charge and although there can be no trial" that it was better for these men to be out of Ireland than to be in it. The Parliamentary Party, opposed upon principle to Sinn Fein, saw that measures such as these meant its ultimate and complete triumph, but no arguments could move the determination of the Government to rely upon force. They seemed to feel that force was the only weapon that was left them and that they might as well use it at once; while Sinn Fein could point to the employment of it as evidence of its own reiterated but constantly challenged contention as to the real attitude of all English Governments towards Ireland. And had the Prime Minister and his advisers, whoever they may have been, deliberately set themselves to prove to Ireland that they were not the wise representatives of an enlightened and friendly democracy (which the Parliamentary Party had up to this represented them to be) but the jealous and implacable guardians of a subject and hated race (which Sinn Fein had always asserted that they were) it is very doubtful whether they could have bettered their record in a single detail. The Parliamentary Party, fighting for its life, with the ground in Ireland slipping from under its feet, appealed pathetically to its old services and old friendship, to the memory of the Irishmen who had fallen in the war, to the opinion of moderate men, to prudence and justice; it could not deflect by one hair's breadth the course chosen by the Cabinet. The fact seems to be that the Tory members who had always hated the Parliamentary Party saw the chance of paying back old scores and embraced it regardless of the consequences; while the Liberals, real and so-called, thought the Parliamentary Party's influence was waning in Ireland, and threw them over without remorse: they had got as much out of them as was to be got, and for the rest they might shift for themselves. It was very difficult to believe that (as the Prime Minister said) the " dominant consideration was the war " and that preoccupation with it was the reason for his refusal to attend to the Irish problem. Everybody knew that Ministers, when they were interested, found time for many other things than the prosecution of the war. What was done and what was not done, and the reasons given both for action and for inaction, only served to deepen the impression of the insincerity of the Cabinet.

Almost simultaneously the Parliamentary Party and Sinn Fein resolved upon an appeal from the English Ministry and the English Parliament to bodies that might be presumed to be less partial. The Irish Party withdrew from Parliament and sent a Manifesto to the United States (now on the verge of its declaration of war) and the self-governing Dominions. Sinn Fein summoned a Convention to meet in Dublin to assert the independence of Ireland, its status as a nation, and its right to representation at the Peace Conference. This was the first, but it was not to be the only, occasion upon which the policy of the Parliamentary Party was moulded, against its will, by the pressure of facts, into a tacit acknowledgment of the justice of the Sinn Fein contention, that parliamentary action was useless. The only difference was that while Sinn Fein held that it always was and always would be useless, English policy being what it always had been, the Parliamentary Party held that the Cabinet had by its action since the Rising destroyed the efficacy of the normally useful and legitimate means of reform.

The effect of this joint appeal from the Cabinet to the impartial opinion of English-speaking countries and belligerent nations was to induce the Prime Minister to bring forward "proposals" for the settlement of the question. He proposed the exclusion of six counties of Ulster from the Home Rule Act, if and when it became operative, the exclusion to be subject to reconsideration after five years; the immediate establishment of an Irish Council (in which the excluded counties were to have the same number of delegates as all the rest of Ireland put together) to legislate for Ireland during the war; and a reconsideration of the financial clauses of the Act. Failing the acceptance of this solution, the Prime Minister saw nothing for it but to summon a representative body of Irishmen to suggest the best means of governing their own country.

The Prime Minister's proposals, whether the product of his own or of some equally ingenious but equally uninformed brain, were promptly rejected by everybody : his concluding suggestion was, after some delay, judged worthy of a trial, the Ulster party stipulating expressly for freedom to refuse to submit to any findings of the Convention with which it did not choose to agree. They were practically informed by the Leader of the House of Commons that their dissent was incompatible with " the substantial agreement" which alone would justify the Government in giving effect to the findings of the Convention.

To claim that the setting up of the Convention was a sincere attempt to solve the problem of Irish Government is to make a demand upon faith which it might be noble, but would certainly be extremely difficult, to grant. The incorporation in the letter by which the Prime Minister suggested it of an official proposal of heads of a settlement could serve no other purpose than to indicate that a particular solution had found favour with the proposer in advance: and to allow the Ulster Party the right of veto was to perpetuate and sanction the attitude which everybody in the Three Kingdoms knew to be the very obstacle which the Convention was blandly invited to surmount. It says much for the general desire of Ireland for peace and settlement that the outcome of the Convention (compassed by secrecy which it was declared a criminal offence to violate while it sat) was awaited generally with an anxious and almost pathetic expectation.

Sinn Fein promptly refused to take any part in the proceedings. It had been formally invited to

# AFTER THE RISING

do so, but as five places only were assigned to it, a number far below that to which its actual strength in the country was known to entitle it, it was not intended that it should have very much weight in the conclusions. Besides, the only solution which it was known to favour, the independence of Ireland, was the only solution which it was not possible for the Convention by the terms of its reference to suggest. In a leader, declining on behalf of the Sinn Fein Party to participate in the proceedings, *Nationality* said, " Ignoring the Convention which is called into being only to distract Ireland from the objective now before her, to confuse her thought, and to permit England to misrepresent her character and her claims to Europe, Sinn Fein summons Ireland to concentrate her mind and energy on preparation for the Peace Conference, where, citing the pledges given to the world by Russia, the United States, and England's Allies, it will invoke that tribunal to judge between our country and her oppressor and claim that the verdict which has restored Poland to independent nationhood shall also be registered for Ireland." The Executive of Sinn Fein also formally and unanimously declined to enter the Convention unless (1) the terms of reference left it free to decree the complete independence of Ireland; (2) the English Government publicly pledged itself to the United States and the Powers of Europe to ratify the decision of the majority of the Convention; (3) the Convention consisted of none but persons freely elected by adult suffrage in Ireland; (4) the treatment of prisoners of war was accorded to Irish political prisoners in English prisons.

Of these proposals the first would have been rejected by the Government, the second by the Ulster Party, and the third by the Parliamentary Party, which by this time was aware that such a method of choosing representatives would leave it almost without representation. The Government to "create an atmosphere" not merely accepted but improved on the fourth condition: the political prisoners were released unconditionally. It is significant of the way in which "atmospheres" are created in Ireland that though the prisoners were released unconditionally on June 17th, a meeting held in Dublin to demand their release, on June 10th, was prohibited by Proclamation, and an attempt to hold it ended in a riot in which a policeman was killed.

While the Convention was preparing to perform the duties which were to end in nothing, Sinn Fein was engaged in the task of rallying the country to its side. The death of Major Willie Redmond had created a vacancy in East Clare: the Parliamentary Party had selected its candidate to succeed him: but in little over a month after the release of the prisoners Mr. de Valera, who had been sentenced to penal servitude for his share in the Rising, was elected by an overwhelming majority. The leader "To the Men of Clare" in which, the week before the election, *Nationality* recommended him to the electors, was suppressed by the Censor. During the same month another vacancy occurred by the death of the member for Kilkenny City, and as a preliminary to the election the authorities suppressed the *Kilkenny People*, the editor of which was chairman of the convention called to select a Sinn Fein candidate, who was promptly returned. Some idea of the appeals which Sinn Fein was making to the electors may be gathered from the leader " To the Electors, Traders and Taxpayers of Kilkenny," in which *Nationality* urged the return of its candidate. It began with a quotation from a memorandum adressed in 1799 to Mr. Pitt by Under-Secretary Cooke, " The Union is the only means of preventing Ireland from becoming too great and too powerful," and by a quotation from another memorandum to the same statesman, " By giving the Irish a hundred members in an assembly of six hundred and fifty they will be impotent to operate upon that assembly, but it will be invested with Irish assent to its authority." Figures were given of the value of the trade between Great Britain and a number of countries in 1914, the trade with Ireland being nearly as valuable as that with the United States, twice that with France and nearly twice that with Germany. It went on : " It will be seen that with the exception of the United States, England has no customer nearly as big as Ireland. . . . . England has had the market to herself for generations ; Sinn Fein proposes that England should not continue to monopolise that market longer. Ireland has £150,000,000

worth of trade to do with the world each year,
£135,000,000 of which is restricted to England. In
return for part of that trade the other countries
of Europe would gladly give Ireland facilities in
their markets and Ireland would compel England
to pay competitive prices. .... So long as
Ireland sends members to the English Parliament
and relies upon that institution, England will
plunder Ireland's revenues and monopolise Ireland's trade at her own price."

Meanwhile the growing popularity of Sinn Fein
was leading to a revival of the Irish Volunteers.
Drilling was resumed and, though frequent arrests
were made and the Government declared its intention at all costs of putting it down, it became more
and more popular. Irish Volunteers even took
possession of the streets of Dublin, in defiance of
military orders, and kept the line of the procession
on the occasion of the funeral of Thomas Ashe who
had died as the result of forcible feeding and
inattention in Mountjoy Prison. Though Sinn
Fein held itself distinct from the Volunteer
Organization it did not refuse to extend some
indirect assistance. It printed a letter of Mr.
Devlin's, addressed from the House of Commons
in July, 1916, to a correspondent, which was
" captured " and read to a Convention of the
National Volunteers in Dublin in August, 1917.
In the letter Mr. Devlin had discouraged the
importation of arms into Ireland for the National
Volunteers, some of whom had assisted the troops
in keeping order during the week of the Rising.

This was of course intended to discredit Mr. Devlin in the eyes of the National Volunteers whose continued allegiance to the Parliamentary Party was now open to grave suspicion. In fact the prospect of their junction with the Irish Volunteers, a highly significant indication of the trend of opinion, decided the Government to disarm them. On the morning of the 15th August every place in which the National Volunteers had stored their arms was raided by the military. The only outcome of this action, combined with the steady and obstinate refusal to seize the arms of the Ulster Volunteers (the only political party in Ireland now left in possession of arms), was to alienate any sympathy remaining for the Government in the ranks of the National Volunteers. Had there been the least pretence of impartiality shown it might have been otherwise : but to disarm all Nationalists of any shade of national politics, while designedly and openly leaving the Unionists armed to the teeth, was a proof, now indeed hardly necessary, of the insincerity of official professions. The disarming of all sections of Nationalists gave an excuse for the practice of raiding for arms which now became common and often led to deplorable results. Innocent people were killed, either designedly or by accident, and the blame for the murders was laid upon the shoulders of Sinn Fein. When a return to the policy of physical force seemed threatened some of the ecclesiastical authorities took alarm, and issued warnings against breaches of the law of God and

resistance to constituted authority. Murder was
of course never countenanced by Sinn Fein: but
as regards resistance to constituted authority, there
were two sides to the question and Sinn Fein was
not at all inclined to allow the ecclesiastical
authorities to dictate its policy. Cardinal Logue
might declare that the Sinn Fein programme was
insane, but it was persisted in without regard to his
opinion. Sinn Fein was always jealous of ecclesiastical interference: it welcomed gladly the co-
operation of ecclesiastics as Irishmen, but it was
determined to keep its own policy in its own hands.

While the Government Convention was sitting
behind closed doors Sinn Fein decided to hold a
Convention of its own, consisting of delegates
freely elected by Sinn Fein Clubs throughout the
country, and to lay its proceedings and conclusions
before the country. The Convention met on
November 1 and unanimously elected Mr. de
Valera as the President of Sinn Fein, a position
which Mr. Griffith had held for six years. The
election was significant: it meant on the one hand
that Sinn Fein thus silently and without any
formal repudiation of its previous constitutional
attitude accepted the Republican programme: it
meant on the other hand that the party of the Rising
now publicly and officially accepted the Sinn Fein
policy and programme as distinct from the policy
of armed insurrection. Mr. de Valera had already
in a reply to the warnings of the bishops denied
that another Rising was in contemplation: he had
also in a speech at Bailieboro' (28th October, 1917),

replied to the kindred charge of pro-Germanism:
" The Sinn Fein Party were said to be pro-
Germans, but if the Germans came to Ireland to
hold it those who are now resisting English power
would be the first to resist the Germans." The
Constitution adopted by the Convention sets out at
great length the policy and objects of Sinn Fein:
its solution of the constitutional problem is as
follows: " Sinn Fein aims at securing the international recognition of Ireland as an independent
Irish Republic. Having achieved that *status* the
Irish people may by referendum freely choose their
own form of government. This object shall be
attained through the Sinn Fein Organization
which shall in the name of the sovereign Irish
People (a) deny the right and oppose the will of
the British Parliament or British Crown or any
other foreign Government to legislate for Ireland;
(b) make use of any and every means available to
render impotent the power of England to hold
Ireland in subjection by military force or otherwise. And whereas no law made without the
authority and consent of the Irish people is, or
ever can be, binding on the Irish people, therefore
in accordance with the resolution of Sinn Fein,
adopted in Convention, 1905, a Constituent
Assembly shall be convoked, comprising persons
chosen by the Irish constituencies, as the supreme
national authority to speak and act in the name
of the Irish people and to devise and formulate
measures for the welfare of the whole people of
Ireland." It will be noticed that the *status* of an

independent Republic is claimed not because
Republicanism is the ideal polity, but because
such a status will leave Ireland free to choose
either that or any other form of government;
further that the new movement expressly links
itself to the Sinn Fein of pre-war days by a formal
recognition of its identity with it and by the
express adoption of its methods; and lastly that
the means by which independence is to be achieved
are defined as " any and every means available,"
the party being pledged neither to nor against any
particular method.

One of the methods upon which Sinn Fein now
relied to achieve success was not the method of
its earlier years. This was frankly acknowledged
by its leaders. In an article on the Convention
summoned by Count Plunkett to meet in the
Mansion House in Dublin after his election for
North Roscommon, *New Ireland* (which was next
to *Nationality* the leading Sinn Fein weekly)
wrote as follows: " In the years 1903—1910 the
policy of Sinn Fein was a policy of self-reliance
in the strictest sense of that term. It directed us
away from Westminster and towards Ireland. It
was revolutionary inasmuch as it sought to dis-
place existing British institutions and substitute
Irish institutions to which the Irish people would
respond. . . . The newer Sinn Fein is not
quite the same as the old: it varies in one essential
characteristic. Whereas the old Sinn Fein
directed the Irish people towards self-improvement
as a basis of national strength and made it quite

## AFTER THE RISING

plain to us that many sacrifices might possibly be demanded, there is no trace in the newer Sinn Fein of these qualities. The older Sinn Fein deprecated the reliance upon any external source of strength and urged upon us the advantages of self-reliance and passive resistance. The new Sinn Fein places some of its faith at least in external bodies and does not inculcate the older doctrine of self-reliance and passive resistance. It is not, however, Sinn Fein that has changed so much as the world forces that condition such changes. The old policy flourished in a period of world peace and was in consequence disposed rather towards a long drawn out struggle: the new policy is specially devised to take advantage of the present temporary state of affairs." This may not be very carefully worded, and it is certain that Sinn Feiners as a body would not have accepted it as a complete and accurate statement of the change in the Sinn Fein programme: but it is a statement (although a careless statement) by a Sinn Fein paper of an important fact—that an appeal to the Peace Conference was not an exercise of "self-reliance" but the adoption for the time of a totally different policy. It was in effect an admission, not that the policy of self-reliance was a failure, but that it had not yet been a success and was not so likely to be successful in the immediate future as an appeal for outside understanding and sympathy. The Parliamentarians had appealed to the sympathy and justice of England: Sinn Fein had declared such an appeal to be futile and had refused to join in it. It was now prepared to issue its own appeal for help and justice not to England but to the Peace Conference. Ever since the Rising the interaction of the two Nationalist parties upon each other's policy had become more and more marked, though they still maintained to one another an attitude of hostility and contempt. If Sinn Fein seemed to change (at any rate for the time) its policy of strict self-reliance into one of an appeal for outside assistance, the Parliamentary Party had shown a disposition no longer to rely upon appeals to English parties and to the English Parliament but to call upon a wider audience to judge its cause. While they still differed upon nearly every other point, they were agreed in this, that to appeal to the Government of 1917 was a waste of time. The appeal to the Peace Conference was destined to fall upon deaf ears but this was not at the time believed to be possible. The Allied statesmen seemed to be committed beyond any possibility of denial or evasion to " the rights of small nations," "government by the consent of the governed" and other formulae of national freedom. In reply to cynical suggestions that these formulae might possibly be discovered to be (to the regret of their authors) inconsistent with the " realities " of politics, *New Ireland* simply answered : " We frankly admit that we have faith and hope in the force of the great moral principle of justice to the nations and in its ultimate power of bringing back order to the chaos and tragedy of Europe and of imposing itself upon reactionaries."

But as a matter of fact, in spite of the energy with which the idea of an appeal to the Peace Conference was taken up and discussed, in spite even of such sweeping statements as that quoted above from *New Ireland*, Sinn Fein had at most agreed to graft a new and temporary policy on to the old stem. It still inculcated self-reliance, the education of the Irish people in questions of national economics, national finance and national policy: it still urged the employment of all the means which could be employed by Irishmen in Ireland to enforce and secure national independence. The columns of *New Ireland* itself make this perfectly plain; and even in later references in that paper to the appeal to the Peace Conference and the hopes founded upon it, the editorial language is much less sweeping than when the idea was fresh in its fascination. The concentration of thought upon the Peace Conference was also exercising in another direction a modifying influence upon Sinn Fein. The old idea of the independence of Ireland was being gradually enlarged. It was no longer confined to the purely negative idea of freedom from foreign control: it assumed the more positive form of an Ireland entering its place in a great community of European nations, equally free and mutually dependent, bound to each other for the preservation of liberty and civilization. It was hoped that the appeal to the Peace Conference would result in the recognition of Ireland not

merely as a nation to which the Conference was
bound to see justice done, but as a brother and
comrade in a new European Confederation for the
advancement of democratic freedom. In this,
Sinn Fein (though the fact is often obscured)
merely represents the form, moulded by special
conditions, which an aspiration, common to many
of the democracies of Europe, had assumed in
Ireland.

The winter of 1917—18 gave Sinn Fein an
opportunity to show that the policy of "self-
reliance" had not been abandoned entirely.
During that winter the shadow of famine hung
over Europe and every nation was engaged in the
effort to avert it from its own shores by rigid con-
servation and economy of its food supply. From
Ireland, under the final control of the English
authorities, food continued to be exported reck-
lessly. Cattle, oats and butter were shipped in
large quantities to England, though it was known
that the food supply of Ireland would barely suffice
for its own necessities till the middle of summer.
The independent and Labour members of the Irish
Food Control Committee protested against this:
but, being a purely advisory body and subject to
the English Food Controller, the Committee found
that all their advice was overruled (as one of
the members put it) "by the man higher up."
The independent members resigned in disgust,
leaving the work of the committee to the officials.
Sinn Fein began at once to organize an unofficial
food census of Ireland: members of the Sinn Fein

Clubs were invited to put at the disposal of the
central organization their local knowledge of the
food supplies of their immediate neighbourhood.
It was the first opportunity on a large scale which
the Republican organization had to show what its
powers and capabilities were and what body of real
support it had in the country. The Chief Council
(Ard-Chomhairle) of Sinn Fein called upon pro-
ducers of, and dealers in, necessary foodstuffs to
" co-operate in the imperative duty of saving Irish
people from starvation by selling only to buyers
for exclusive Irish use": it urged the workers in
the country, on the railways and at the ports, to
refuse to co-operate in the exportation of food and
called upon the public to treat food exporters as
common enemies. The Food Committee established
by the Sinn Fein Council sent circulars to the
clergy of all denominations soliciting their help
both in conserving the food supply and in making
suitable arrangements for its distribution. It was
not very easy either to secure a food census or to
induce those who made money by the export of
food to forego their profits. The principal export
of potatoes was from Antrim, Down, Derry and
Tyrone, counties in which Sinn Fein had very
little prospect either of getting the requisite information from the farmers or of inducing them to
forego their profits. English dealers were willing
to pay large prices for Irish produce and Irish
farmers were apparently willing to go on selling
until, as *New Ireland* put it, there would be
nothing left in Ireland to eat except bank notes

The situation was in all essentials what it had been during the closing years of the eighteenth century when (as Arthur O'Connor pointed out) Ireland was supplying the belligerents of Europe with food and leaving her own population to starve, while the traders waxed wealthy. The only difference was that, the inducement then being a bounty paid by Parliament on exported corn, the inducement now was a bounty paid by the purchaser in England in the form of an enhanced price. It was a situation which, as the Labour Party was quick to point out, could not be met by any unofficial organization however energetic, such as the Sinn Fein Food Committee, but required official action. The Labour Party demanded that the Irish Food Control Committee should be strengthened and vested with executive powers, no longer remaining subordinate to the London Controller: until this was done, private or unofficial advice or action was merely playing with the question. Whether Sinn Fein exerted any but a slight influence on the export of food may be doubted; but it certainly managed the other part of its task—the distribution of the available supplies—with a certain skill. Measures were concerted for purchasing supplies in counties where food was relatively abundant and sending it to agents in districts where it was scarce. The usual abuses which attend attempts to supply food to a poor population could not, of course, be entirely eliminated, but on the whole the experiment seems to have been generally successful. In Ennis, for instance, the local Sinn Fein Club established a Sinn Fein market to which farmers brought their potatoes: the club purchased them at the current price and distributed them to 150 poor families at cost: each family was provided with a card endorsed with the quantity of potatoes necessary for its needs and on presentation of the card received the potatoes. The scheme was financed by some prominent men in Ennis who advanced the necessary capital, the Sinn Fein Club being at the cost of the working expenses of the scheme: there was "no credit and no charity." Although this and similar schemes worked fairly well, and undoubtedly relieved the situation appreciably in many districts, they were open to the objection brought by the Labour Party that they were ineffective as compared both with genuine co-operative effort on the part of the people themselves and with official action taken by the County Councils or municipal authorities. They were, besides, likely to give rise to the question which *Irish Opinion* (the Irish Labour weekly) put " Is the object political or economic?" There is no doubt that the fact that Sinn Fein was actively promoting measures of relief, while official action tended to produce a situation approaching to famine, was used as an argument in favour of the Sinn Fein policy in general. It was hardly to be expected either that Sinn Feiners should not use the argument or that the public should not think that there was something in it. The Labour Party's criticisms were, from the economic point of view, perfectly sound. An Irish Food Control

Committee with executive powers, authority in the
hands of locally-elected bodies to conserve and
distribute local supplies of food, was ideally the
proper scheme: but the proper scheme was, as
usual, unattainable and Sinn Fein was doing what
was perhaps the only thing that could be done
under the circumstances. And though the Labour
Party urged its criticisms, it did not withhold its
assistance and hearty support to the Sinn Fein
scheme.

The result was to increase the growing popularity of Sinn Fein. It was seen that it had
another than the purely political aspect, that its
principles of self-reliance were capable of being
applied with a success limited only by the amount
of popular support which they could command.
It was, at any rate, plain that if the people who
controlled the food supplies were all believers in
Sinn Fein principles there need be no prospect of
famine in Ireland, and the action of Sinn Fein
(inadequate though it may have been) at any rate
contrasted favourably with the indifference and
inefficiency of the official bodies appointed by the
Government and with the helplessness of other
political parties.

The popularity of Sinn Fein was further in-
increased by the continued activities of the Irish
police authorities against its more prominent or
active adherents. If the Cabinet had decided to
create an "atmosphere" for the Convention by
the release of the prisoners sentenced to penal
servitude for their share in the Rising, an

opposite "atmosphere" was being systematically generated by the Irish Executive. People were being arrested all over the country for offences incomparably less serious from every point of view than those committed by the people who had been released. The conclusion was drawn that the Government, while anxious to make a display to the world of impartiality and good will by a spectacular act of clemency, was in reality determined to regard the active support of Sinn Fein as a serious offence in the case of men too little before the eyes of the world for their arrest to lead to widespread comment or indignation. Their action was held to be an indication of their resolve to prevent the spread of Sinn Fein principles until the Convention should have presented a report palatable to the Cabinet: and Sinn Fein instead of suffering by this action simply grew in its own esteem and in the eyes of others.

The result of the South Armagh Election early in 1918, in which its candidate was defeated, only spurred Sinn Fein to further exertions. The election indicated more a desire " to give the Convention a chance" than a deliberate judgment of the electorate in favour of the Parliamentary as against the Sinn Fein policy. But a " chance given" to the Convention was in reality an opportunity denied to Sinn Fein. The Convention was to produce a scheme for the government of Ireland " within the Empire." A tolerable and workable scheme produced unanimously (or nearly so) by the Convention would undoubtedly (or so it was

thought) have to be accepted by the Cabinet; if
such a scheme were accepted and put into operation, the feeling of relief in Ireland would have
been so deep and so general as to deal to Sinn
Fein, just when it was beginning to gain the ear
of the country, a blow from which it might take
long to recover, if it should recover it for a
generation. It was felt that a Sinn Fein victory
in South Armagh would mean that the Convention
might for all practical purposes adjourn indefinitely, while a victory for the Parliamentary
Party meant that it was given the opportunity,
so far as Nationalist Ireland represented by this
constituency was concerned, of producing a scheme
of self-government wide enough to win the support of all Irishmen really desirous of a reasonable
step in advance.

Sinn Fein decided in the circumstances to put
the real opinion of Ireland on the question of
independence to a definite test before the Convention should have time to report in favour of something attractive to moderate men, if offered, but
falling short of independence. On St. Patrick's
Day "monster meetings" were held all over Ireland, attended by the Volunteers who mustered in
force and by crowds which were certainly enthusiastic. At all of these meetings the following
resolution was put in Irish and in English and,
according to the reports, passed everywhere with
practical unanimity: " Here on St. Patrick's Day
we join with our fellow-countrymen at home and
in foreign lands in proclaiming once more that

Ireland is a distinct nation whose just right is sovereign independence. This right has been asserted in every generation, has never been surrendered and never allowed to lapse. We call the nations to witness that to-day as in the past it is by force alone that England holds Ireland for her Empire and not by the consent of the Irish; and that England's claim to have given the Irish people 'self-determination' is a lie: her true attitude being shown by the recent ministerial statement that 'under no circumstances could any English Government contemplate the ultimate independence of Ireland'." In Dublin, Belfast and Clare these meetings were proclaimed and could not be held—at least on the appointed day. In Belfast Mr. de Valera addressed the meeting at 11 o'clock on the night preceding, but when midnight struck the gathering was dispersed by the police. But a "monster meeting" is a thing of varying dimensions: even "monster meetings" held simultaneously all over Ireland may not be attended by more than a fraction of the population. To put the matter beyond doubt it was decided to institute a plebiscite in favour of independence and to publish the numbers who in each townland declared themselves in favour of it. While the plebiscite was being taken Sinn Fein had again an opportunity of "testing the feeling of the country" at a parliamentary election. Mr. John Redmond had died on the 6th of March. He had fought for his policy to the last with tenacity and dignity: through a long life he had displayed the courage which once

led the small and faithful band who refused to
betray Parnell: he had come to accept the limitations imposed upon his policy by English feeling
with a pride which preferred to regard them as the
dictates of statesmanship: he never lost his
courtesy, his confidence or his belief in human
sincerity. To Sinn Fein he had opposed an un-
bending hostility, and the temptation to replace
him in the representation of Waterford by a Sinn
Feiner was too great to be resisted. Sinn Fein
sustained a heavy defeat at the poll, and this second
reverse within a few months was taken to indicate
the turning of the tide in favour of Mr. Redmond's
policy. It really meant no more than that the
electors of Waterford thought, what many other
people thought with them, that the attempt to oust
Mr. Redmond's son from sitting for his father's
constituency was a breach of the decencies of public
life. Certainly the language which some of the
party used in speaking of Mr. Redmond was inex-
cusable and deserved the rebuff which it received.

But the report of the Convention, laid upon the
table of the House of Commons early in April,
overshadowed plebiscites and the results of contested elections. Upon its reception by the
Government the whole future of Ireland seemed
to turn. But the report was difficult to master.
The Chairman of the Convention claimed that it
had "laid a foundation of Irish agreement unprecedented in history," but the actual record of the
proceedings seemed at first blush open to a somewhat different interpretation. The Nationalists

had, it is true, offered large concessions to the
Unionists, but they were themselves divided upon
questions of principle of the very first importance;
and while some of the Unionists were content to
accept what was offered, provided the Nationalists
met the concession of this acceptance by a concession infinitely greater, the Ulster Unionists appeared to have succeeded in committing themselves
to nothing. If the Government were to attempt
to legislate for Ireland on the basis of the report
the Ulster Unionists were certain to produce the
" pledges" that they would not be " coerced" and
too many responsible people had given these
pledges to make the prospect of legislation for Ireland a comfortable outlook for anybody. But not
only was the report difficult to interpret, not only
did its publication put Ministers in an awkward
position: it came at a most unfortunate time. The
military prospects of the Allies were clouded, and
the Government had decided to make a fresh call
upon the man-power of the country. It was
known that in their perplexity they had considered
the possibility of extending Conscription to Ireland, and to do so, equally with refraining from
doing so, seemed to be a step of doubtful
expediency.

The situation was complicated; but the handling
of it by the Prime Minister was more complicated
still. He elected to treat the question of Home
Rule and the question of Irish Conscription con-
currently while he declared that they were not
interdependent. He justified the application of

Conscription to Ireland on the merits: men were needed in France and there were men to be had in Ireland: the Home Rule Act, accepted by the Parliamentary Party and placed on the Statute Book, had given to Parliament the right to legislate for Ireland upon matters of Imperial concern. As for the Convention, he refused to regard the report as disclosing that there had been "substantial agreement," nevertheless he announced that the Government would bring forward immediately such proposals for the future government of Ireland as seemed to be just. It was common belief that so far as the Convention was concerned a failure to arrive at " substantial agreement" absolved the Government from all obligation to legislate upon its proposals; an intention of legislating all the same appeared to be prompted by the desire to offer something in the way of compensation for the unpalatable proposal of Conscription. But the Premier insisted that any such interpretation of his proposal was erroneous: the two measures had nothing whatever to do with one another: each stood upon its own merits and each must be passed regardless of the other. But, having elected to take Conscription first, and having announced his intention of forcing it through Parliament in spite of criticism and of putting it into operation in Ireland in spite of opposition, he indulged himself in a glimpse at the prospects of a conscribed Ireland: " when the young men of Ireland," he said, " have been brought in large numbers into the fighting line, it is important that they should

## AFTER THE RISING

feel that they are not fighting for the purpose of establishing a principle abroad which is denied to them at home." But as if in fear that this might imply some remote connection between Ireland's duty to fight and Ireland's right to be given the benefit of the principle it was asked to fight for, the Premier gave the most convincing proof of his sincerity in saying that Conscription for Ireland and Home Rule for Ireland did not "stand together"—Conscription was passed into law and Home Rule was dropped.

It is difficult to conceive a course of action more nicely calculated to demonstrate on a large scale the principal theses which Sinn Fein had been preaching for years. The demonstration was carried into every household in Ireland in a form in which it could no longer be ignored. Conscription had not been a palatable measure in England, and it had not been put into force until the English people had agreed with practical unanimity that they must submit to it: but the choice had been their own and no Government would have ventured even to propose it until the English people had made up their minds beforehand to accept it when it should be proposed. In Australia it had been discussed and rejected; and no one either in England or anywhere else had questioned the right of the people of Australia to decline to conscribe themselves, though the interests of Australia were as vitally involved in the issue of the war as the interests of England. Ireland, on the other hand, while it was opposed to Conscription, had no choice offered to it in the matter. It was decided upon by a Cabinet of which no Irishman was a member and it was to be enforced in spite not merely of the protests of Ireland but of the grave warnings of a large number of Englishmen. To the argument that Ireland, being an integral part of the United Kingdom, must submit to the legislation of Parliament whether it liked it or no, it was pointed out that this argument had not been enforced against Ulster four years before; that when Conscription had first been enforced in England it had been admitted by Parliament that Ireland was a special case; that to assert that Ireland was an integral part of the United Kingdom was to beg the very question in dispute, since the national claim of Ireland had always been a claim for independence. Again, if the Home Rule Act was relied upon (as the Premier relied upon it) to prove that Ireland had accepted the authority of Parliament in Imperial matters and acknowledged its supreme jurisdiction in all matters pertaining to war and peace, it was pointed out that the Government which now invoked it had persistently refused to put it into operation. Yet the Premier, who, more than any other single man, had shown himself hostile in deed, while friendly in word, to Irish claims, himself admitted that Irishmen serving in the army in the then condition of Irish affairs would be fighting abroad to enforce a principle denied in the government of their own country. The conclusion which Sinn Fein drew was that the English Government was prepared in defiance of public feeling, justice and constitutional practice to enforce Conscription upon Ireland by naked force: that it had no intention of granting Ireland any form of self-government, and that it was the duty of Irishmen to organize " an effective and protracted resistance." But, though prepared to resist, it continued to argue. It pointed out that the Irish Parliament, whose powers had been transferred by the Act of Union to the Parliament of England, had possessed no power of Conscription and could not transfer a power which it did not possess; any power of Conscription, therefore, possessed by Parliament over Ireland must rest upon some other basis, if it existed at all: that there was no legal process by which a man could be deprived of life or liberty except on conviction for a crime: and that this was why, even in the case of Conscription in England, Mr. Asquith, a good constitutional lawyer, " was careful to declare that he based the conscription of Englishmen on the basis, not of State duty or compulsion, but of the universal assent of the English people." If this assent was lacking, as it undoubtedly was, in the case of Ireland, it followed that to enforce Conscription was an act of naked injustice.

But no elaborate argument was needed to rouse a people convinced at last that they were in the vortex of Charybdis. They resented what now appeared as the duplicity with which for months their attention had been deliberately and elaborately focussed upon the alluring mysteries of the

Convention while they drifted quietly and securely towards the edge of the whirlpool. They saw the cloudy structure of the Convention melt and float away, disclosing what it had covered; and they prepared for a desperate struggle.

The feeling was not confined to Sinn Fein. The Parliamentary Party left Westminster in a body and crossed to Ireland to help in the national resistance. The Labour Party joined hands with them and with Sinn Fein in the universal crisis. It involved for the Parliamentary Party a tragic and fatal break with the past. It was the end of all their hopes, of all their influence, of their very existence; and as they joined the Sinn Fein and Labour representatives round the table of the Mansion House Conference, summoned by the Lord Mayor of Dublin, they must have felt that they were invited by virtue of what they had once been rather than by virtue of what they were; they were there as the men who had relied on the broken reed, "whereon if a man lean it will go into his hand and pierce him."

After its first meeting on April 18th, the Mansion House Conference issued the following declaration:—" Taking our stand on Ireland's separate and distinct nationhood and affirming the principle of liberty that the Governments of nations derive their just powers from the consent of the governed, we deny the right of the British Government or any external authority to impose compulsory military service in Ireland against the clearly expressed will of the Irish people. The passing of the Conscription Bill by the British House of Commons must be regarded as a declaration of war on the Irish nation. The alternative to accepting it as such is to surrender our liberties and to acknowledge ourselves slaves. It is in direct violation of the rights of small nationalities to self-determination, which even the Prime Minister of England—now preparing to employ naked militarism and force his Act upon Ireland— himself officially announced as an essential condition for peace at the Peace Congress. The attempt to enforce it will be an unwarrantable aggression, which we call upon all Irishmen to resist by the most effective means at their disposal." On the same day the Conference decided to ask the co-operation of the Irish Catholic Bishops who had been summoned by Cardinal Logue to meet at Maynooth. The Bishops, after hearing a deputation from the Mansion House Conference, issued at once the following manifesto: "An attempt is being made to force Conscription on Ireland against the will of the Irish nation and in defiance of the protests of its leaders. In view especially of the historic relations between the two countries from the very beginning up to this moment, we consider that Conscription forced in this way upon Ireland is an oppressive and inhuman law, which the Irish people have a right to resist by every means that are consonant with the law of God. We wish to remind our people that there is a higher Power which controls the affairs of men. They have in their hands the means of conciliating that Power by strict adherence to the Divine law, by more earnest attention to their religious duties, and by fervent and persevering prayer. In order to secure the aid of the Holy Mother of God, who shielded our people in the days of their greatest trials, we have already sanctioned a National Novena in honour of Our Lady of Lourdes, commencing on the 3rd May, to secure general and domestic peace. We also exhort the heads of families to have the Rosary recited every evening with the intention of protecting the spiritual and temporal welfare of our beloved country and bringing us safe through this crisis of unparalleled gravity."

Many Sinn Feiners sincerely deplored the step which the Conference had taken in calling upon the Bishops for an official manifesto. Its wording seemed to rule out of existence the section of Irish Nationalists who belonged to the Protestant faith and to identify a national question with a particular creed. Certainly as a mere question of tactics the manifesto was of doubtful wisdom. It was certain to raise, and it did raise, the cry of the "priest in politics." From the mouths of the Ulster Party the criticism might be disregarded, for they had themselves four years before induced the Protestant churches in Ulster to pass official resolutions against Home Rule. But it was different when the English newspapers began to raise the "No Popery" cry and to write as if Sinn Fein were a purely Catholic party which it had never ceased to protest it was not. But in fact the vexed question of the relation of the Church to the civil power, a question not to be disposed of in a sentence, did not fairly arise from the Bishops' pronouncement. The main gist of it was contained in two propositions neither of which was theological: the proposition that Conscription was an oppressive and inhuman law was (whether right or wrong) an ordinary statement of opinion upon a purely mundane matter: the proposition that such a law might be resisted by any means consonant with the law of God was the statement not of theology, whether Catholic or Protestant, but of ordinary ethics, accidentally theistic. But the concluding sentences of the manifesto threw their light backwards upon the essential statements, and the resistance to Conscription was represented as one more incident in the long struggle between free institutions and the power of the Roman Church.

Nationalist Ireland, however, needed no incentive from the Bishops to resist. It was presented with a clear cut issue which could not be evaded, which the Cabinet by its decision had raised in its most acute form. If Ireland submitted quietly to Conscription then it acknowledged that it stood to the British Parliament in exactly the same relation as did Yorkshire or Middlesex: if, on the other hand, Ireland were a nation, even if it were a nation within the British Empire, it had the right to decide for itself on a question involving issues so vital to its future. This was the alternative which Sinn Fein put in vehement and passionate language before the country and the reply of Nationalist Ireland was practically unanimous. Nearly every Nationalist in Ireland took the anti-Conscription pledge " Denying the right of the British Government to enforce compulsory service in this country, we pledge ourselves solemnly to one another to resist Conscription by the most effective means at our disposal."

But not only was the intention of the Government to enforce Conscription regarded as a challenge to Ireland, as a denial of its nationality; a deeper purpose was supposed to lie behind it. The record of the Government during the war in its dealings with Ireland had not been such as to persuade Nationalists of any section that it was either friendly or sincere. It was believed that, coupled with the desire to obtain recruits, and the intention of treating the Irish claim to a national existence as a thing of no consequence in order to secure them, there was the desire further to deplete Ireland of its Nationalist population and render its government by England easier in consequence. This belief did not always find public expression, but it existed and had much to do with the vehemence of the resistance. Apart from this consideration, the motives of the opposition and the feelings with which it was connected were succinctly given by *New Ireland*. "At the basis of the opposition to Conscription stand the moral rights of Ireland, the very rock as it were of Irish nationality, the rights to choose her own future and to protect her people from the horrors of the European War. If there were any statesmanship left in England to-day it would look to creating harmony between Ireland and England, knowing that the real interest of nations is built thereon. Real statesmanship would grant Ireland the fullest liberty, knowing that the friendship of Ireland is essential, and that it can only be based on the fundamentals of national honour, namely, liberty and justice. Instead English politicians vainly imagine that coercion, the press gang, and the train of consequent tragedy will somehow win the allegiance and support of Ireland."

The most spectacular demonstration of protest was made by the Irish Labour Party. A conference of fifteen hundred delegates convened in Dublin by the Irish Trades Union Congress, in adopting a resolution to resist Conscription " in every way that to us seems feasible," asserting " our claims for independent status as a nation in the international movement and the right of self-determination as a nation as to what action or actions our people should take on questions of political or economic issues," called upon Irish workers to abstain from all work on April 23rd as "a demonstration of fealty to the cause of Labour and Ireland." This was the first occasion in Western Europe on which it had been decided to call a general national strike: and the strike in Ireland was general except in North-east Ulster. The Labour Party however had a point of view somewhat different from that of Sinn Fein. Labour was opposed to Conscription on principle, and would have, unlike Sinn Fein, opposed it even if agreed to by an Irish Parliament. Their view had been clearly expressed more than a year before when, after two years of silence, Irish Labour began again to publish a weekly paper. *Irish Opinion* in its first number, published on December 1st, 1917, had said, " We shall resolutely oppose the conscription of Irish people, whether for military or industrial purposes. The very idea of compulsory service is abhorrent to us and we shall assist in every way every effort of our people to resist the imposition of such an iniquitous system upon us."

However neither minor differences on the subject of Conscription nor, indeed, major differences upon other points, prevented all sections of Nationalist opinion from assisting each other heartily in the crisis. A common statement of Ireland's case against Conscription was drawn up for publication and the Lord Mayor of Dublin was deputed to proceed to America to lay the protest of Ireland before the President of the United States. The Government showed no signs of yielding to the opposition. The Lord Lieutenant known to be opposed to the policy of the Cabinet was recalled, and his place was taken by Field Marshal Lord French with whom Mr. Shortt was appointed Chief Secretary, one of a considerable number of " English Home Rulers" who have at various times been appointed to the post of Chief Secretary for Ireland by virtue of their profession of the belief that no such post should be permitted to exist, and whose conduct in it has been such as might be expected from such persons. It was announced with official emphasis that no opposition would deflect the Government from its purpose. The Lord Mayor of Dublin was refused permission to leave Ireland until he should first have submitted for the approval of Lord French the memorial which he was charged to

## AFTER THE RISING

convey to the President of the United States. But nothing altered the opposition to Conscription, and the Government had to be content with the suspension of the sword.

When the formidable nature of the task they had undertaken dawned upon the Lord Lieutenant and his Chief Secretary, it was decided by the Irish Government to cut the sinews of the opposition by the arrest of those who were chiefly responsible for fomenting it. But it was clearly impossible to clap the Catholic Bishops and the Mansion House Conference into gaol in a body. It was plain that Sinn Fein was the chief centre of the trouble, being the only political party whose principles furnished a logical ground for opposition to the conscription of Ireland by Act of Parliament. The two Sinn Fein members of the Mansion House Conference, Messrs. de Valera and Griffith, with a number of less prominent Sinn Feiners, were deported and imprisoned. But this was a course which required some explanation. They were not the only people prominent in the Anti-Conscription campaign; and in any case English public opinion while, on the whole, indignant with the attitude of Ireland towards compulsory service, was becoming somewhat uneasy as to happenings in Ireland and inclined to question the entire wisdom of the Irish Executive. Accordingly, it was asserted that the arrested Sinn Feiners had been guilty of complicity in a German plot. The ex-Lord Lieutenant, Lord Wimborne, during whose tenure of office the discovery of the plot (it was said) began to be made, publicly and flatly denied all knowledge of

it, and expressed disbelief in its existence. The
Premier announced that he had seen the evidence
(which nothing, however, would induce him to
divulge) and that it was even as the Irish Government had said. Public opinion however was still
unsatisfied, and the Irish office issued a statement
on the subject in which the Chief Secretary argued
("for even though vanquished he could argue
still") from the history of Sinn Fein for the previous three or four years, and from certain financial
transactions between Count Bernstorff and some
Irish-Americans before America entered the war,
that some person or persons in Ireland had been in
communication with Germany for a treasonable
purpose. However that may have been, there was
no direct evidence connecting any of the prisoners
with any of these transactions, and in fact nearly
all of them had been in gaol in England at the time
when the transactions took place. The official
statement was pitilessly analysed in a pamphlet
published by *New Ireland* entitled " The Plot:
German or English?" the only result of the whole
affair being that official credit in Ireland received
its last shock. No further attempts were made to
provide non-political reasons for political arrests:
it was judged better that the Executive should rely
upon the extraordinary powers conferred upon it
by the Defence of the Realm Act (though the
machinery provided by what was known as " the
ordinary law" in Ireland seemed sufficiently complete without it) to arrest, without the necessity of
charge or trial, any persons who made themselves
prominent for the advocacy of Sinn Fein or Repub-

## AFTER THE RISING

lican politics. In July Sinn Fein, the **Gaelic League, Cumann na mBan** and the **Irish Volunteers** were declared to be "dangerous associations" to which Irish men and women would in future belong at their own risk. Concerts, hurling matches, literary competitions, were prohibited all over Ireland by military force when they were held under the auspices of persons politically obnoxious to the Government. Government became a matter of having enough troops in the country to ensure that the Executive was able to do precisely what it pleased. Ireland was treated frankly as hostile and occupied territory, and the last pretence of constitutional government was finally abandoned.

The reply of Sinn Fein to the arrest of Mr. Griffith for complicity in the " German Plot" had been his triumphant election for East Cavan. This was almost the last seat which the once powerful Parliamentary Party ventured to contest. Its co-operation with Sinn Fein in the question of Conscription had been, not an alliance but an operation conducted in common, and on other points each was at perfect liberty to pursue its own path. But the junction of forces had only succeeded in bringing into clear relief the essential incompatibility of the Sinn Fein and the Parliamentary policies, and it became evident that the Irish public would have to choose definitely which it should finally adopt. Sinn Fein, which refused to compromise on the essential principle of Ireland's distinct and independent nationhood, could argue with considerable force that on this assumption alone could

Ireland object to Conscription with confidence and moral justification—that if Ireland were not a nation, but a province or a dependency, then the resistance to Conscription was legally and morally without a sound basis. It was extremely difficult for the Parliamentary Party to counter this argument: and in point of fact some of them did not try to counter it but frankly dissociated themselves from the Anti-Conscription policy. It was perfectly clear that the Home Rule Act reserved such powers to Parliament as to make the conscription of Ireland, as part of a general measure of Conscription for the United Kingdom, a step which Parliament would legally be entitled to take and which, once the Home Rule Act was accepted by Ireland as satisfactory (and the Parliamentary Party had declared that it was) Ireland would have no moral right to resist. The Party began to shift its ground: it could no longer, in view of Irish feeling, remain advocates of a settlement which made Conscription possible: it would not go the whole way with Sinn Fein and declare that no settlement would be satisfactory which did not acknowledge the right of Ireland to independent nationhood, to self-determination and the right to choose its own form of government. The Party settled down unofficially to the advocacy of a form of Home Rule which should ensure to Ireland piecemeal and in detail, by enactment of Parliament, as large an independence as was possessed by the self-governing Dominions, without the formal and definite renunciation of the right of Parliament to decide the extent to which Ireland should be independent. This of course left the question of principle precisely where it was. But on the question of principle Sinn Fein was adamant, and Nationalist Ireland supported Sinn Fein by an overwhelming majority.

The relationship between Sinn Fein and the Hierarchy was more enigmatic and gave rise to much speculation. One view was that Sinn Fein had 'captured' the Hierarchy, another was that the Hierarchy had 'captured' Sinn Fein. Neither view was, of course, correct. Individual bishops may have sympathized (individual priests certainly sympathized in large numbers) with Sinn Fein: but it is certain that quite a large number of priests and bishops did not. While it is true that resistance to Conscription could not logically be justified except upon the principles of Sinn Fein, bishops had the same right to be illogical as members of the Parliamentary Party. Under the stress of the moment, in the desire to save their flocks from the danger that threatened them, they had joined forces with a party which before that they had not approved of and which they were not bound to approve of afterwards. Sinn Fein, at any rate, was under no illusion as to the feelings of some of the Bishops. The curate of Crossna, Father O'Flanagan, had taken a very active part on the side of Sinn Fein in the East Cavan election. Shortly afterwards he was deprived by his bishop, the Most Rev. Dr. Coyne, of all his faculties as a priest, including the right to say Mass. The technical offence for which he was punished in this way was that of having addressed meetings within the boundaries of three parishes in Cavan without first obtaining the permission of the local parish priests. Everybody knew that the real reason for his punishment was not the technical offence but the fact that his speeches had been strongly (and even violently) Sinn Fein. The people of Crossna retorted by shutting up the parish church and refusing to allow Mass to be said in it by anyone else. *Nationality,* in reporting the facts, said of Father O'Flanagan: " He has been condemned to the most harsh judgment that can be meted out to a priest by his bishop and until that wrong has been set right Sinn Fein will stand by Father O'Flanagan"; and practically every Sinn Feiner in Ireland agreed with these words. When bishops seemed (as many of them did) to go out of their way to criticise in pastorals and public letters the policy or the tactics of Sinn Fein, their action was resented and openly, even stringently, criticised in the Sinn Fein papers: but all this was done not only without any trace of anti-clericalism (in the proper sense of the word) but with what sometimes seemed an almost exaggerated deference to the office and sacred functions of the bishop as such. As a matter of fact the Catholic Church in Ireland during the nineteenth century has always been on the side of law and order. It has had a strong bias towards constituted authority, as was to be expected from a branch of the most conservative institution in the world. It excommunicated the Fenians, it opposed the Land League, it condemned the Rising. It is hardly too much to say that Ireland would have been un-

governable but for the influence of the Church.
It raised its voice against outrage and murder in
language beside which the denunciations of
politicians sound tame and flaccid. If it has
meddled in politics (as it has) it has done no more
than the Protestant Churches in Ireland, every
one of which is " in politics" up to the neck.

And the co-operation of Labour and Sinn Fein
in the opposition to Conscription by no means
meant either that Labour had become Sinn Fein
or that Sinn Fein had adopted the Labour programme. In fact its relation to Labour is a
problem which Sinn Fein has been very long in
solving. The alliance between Republican
Volunteers and the Citizen Army in the Rising
effected no more than a temporary and partial
union. The very first number of *Irish Opinion*
had some very open criticism of the attitude
of Sinn Fein to Irish Labour. The Sinn Fein
Convention of November 1st, 1917, had passed
two Labour resolutions, one of which affirmed the
right of Labour to a " fair and reasonable" wage:
the other was in favour of Irish Labour severing
its connection with British Trades Unions. On
the first of these *Irish Opinion* remarked: " The
resolution of the Sinn Fein Convention conceding
to Irish Labour the right to fair and reasonable
wages was not by any means encouraging. It was
a resolution to which the assent of even Mr. W.
M. Murphy might have been secured. It did not
go far enough, and it bore upon the face of it
timidity and trepidation. The Labour demand
to-day goes rather beyond fair and reasonable

wages: the British Government is prepared to
offer, in fact has actually offered, some share in
direction to British Labour. This being so, there
is not much to be gained from Mr. de Valera's
statement in his Mansion House speech 'that in a
free Ireland, with the social conditions that
obtained in Ireland, Labour had a far better chance
than it would have in capitalist England.' ' Our
Labour policy,' continued Mr. de Valera, ' is a
policy of a free country, and we ask Labour to
join with us to free the country. We recognize
that we can never free it without Labour. And
we say, when Labour frees this country—helps to
free it—Labour can look for its own share of its
patrimony.' We agree that ' to free the country'
is an object worthy of all the devotion that men
can give to it, but at the same time we would
urge that, pending this devoutly-to-be-wished-for
consummation, men and women must live and rear
the families upon which the future Ireland
depends. What Mr. de Valera asks in effect is that
Labour should wait till freedom is achieved before
it claims ' its share of its patrimony.' There are
free countries, even Republics, where Labour
claims ' its share in its patrimony' in vain. We
can work for freedom, and we will, but at the
same time we'll claim our share of our patrimony
when and where opportunity offers." This is to
put the issue squarely. Labour was not going to
commit itself blindfold to any policy of "ignoring"
indiscriminately all " English law," when by
recognizing it any practical advantage was to be
gained. Labour had too keen an eye to the

realities of life to refuse a gift from the left hand because the right hand had smitten it or picked its pocket. It was prepared to settle its account with the owner of both hands when opportunity offered, but, for the present, "a man must live." "Fleshpots or Freedom" might form an attractive motto for the front page of *New Ireland*, but Labour saw no virtue (since Freedom's back was turned anyhow) in leaving the pots untasted on a point of honour. The resolution calling upon Irish Labour to withdraw from association with English Labour was flatly ignored. Irish Labour was, and intended to remain, international: it was not going to refuse co-operation with Labour in France or Belgium —it appointed delegates to the Stockholm Conference—and it saw no reason to refuse co-operation with Labour in England. Besides, without the help of English Labour it felt unable to stand alone. And Labour, while it sympathized with the demand for Irish independence, did not wish to commit itself to any step which would make it more difficult than it need be to win the co-operation of the Unionist workingmen of Belfast and the North. Curiously enough, while Sinn Fein was calling upon Irish Labour to withdraw from membership of English Trades Unions, the Unionist leaders in Ulster were trying to induce Belfast Labour to do the same thing: but while Sinn Fein objected to the English Labour Party because it was English, the Ulster politicians objected to it because it was in favour of Home Rule. Among the Sinn Fein papers, *New Ireland*, while faithful to the resolution of the Convention, saw most clearly the reasons which explained the Labour attitude and, while expressing the hope that a severance from the English Unions would eventually occur, pleaded for toleration and for, in the meantime, a free hand for Labour.

But the Sinn Fein difficulty in regard to Labour lay deeper than any mere question of tactics. The leaders of Irish Labour might be Republicans, but they were also largely Socialists, and where Socialism is suspected the Church has to be reckoned with. James Connolly, the revered leader of Irish Labour, had been (though he died a sincere Catholic) supposed to have come into conflict with the Church for his opinions on social questions. His associate, James Larkin, had more than once furnished a text for some very plain speaking in pastorals and from the altar for the alleged subversive and immoral tendency of his teaching on Labour questions. During the General Election of 1918 a sentence from James Connolly's writings, which had been quoted on a Sinn Fein election poster, was the subject of a bitter and prolonged controversy, during which Sinn Fein was challenged by a militant Churchman either to repudiate Connolly's political philosophy or to declare itself opposed to the authoritative teaching of the Church. Sinn Fein, very wisely, did neither: but it was felt very generally that while this might be wisdom for the moment, it was not wisdom for all time: and Sinn Fein has still to formulate its social philosophy.

The conclusion of the war made no difference in the government of Ireland except that more troops

## AFTER THE RISING

might be expected to be available for the maintenance of law and order. Martial law was not relaxed or revoked: the Competent Military Authority retained unimpaired over large areas of Ireland the power to arrest and imprison (often for long periods) persons charged with every variety of offence which could be interpreted as dangerous to the prestige and efficiency of that form of government which is best administered under the sanction of a courtmartial. Men, women and children were arrested upon charges not specified and committed to prison for periods impossible to ascertain either from the authorities who sent them, or the authorities who kept them, there. It was under such circumstances that Ireland was asked to take part in the Victory Election of 1918. The electors of Great Britain were asked to give a " mandate" to the British representatives at the Peace Conference, and "to strengthen their hands" in exacting from the Central Empires and their Allies the full measure of punishment. Ireland decided to give a " mandate" which was neither asked for nor desired and to " strengthen the hands" of the Peace Plenipotentiaries in demanding that for which the war had ostensibly been fought—the freedom of small nations. It was known that the Parliamentary Party would retain only a fraction of the seats it once held and that Sinn Fein would be in a majority. For a time it seemed as if the verdict of the majority might be weakened by the intrusion of Labour candidates who, though most of them were Sinn Feiners in point of fact and all of them were bound by the

Labour Party not to attend Parliament except
when ordered by the Labour Congress, would give
no pledge of absolute and rigid abstention from the
English Parliament and were Labour candidates
first and Sinn Feiners afterwards. At one time it
seemed as if an acute conflict between Sinn Fein
and Labour might occur. But the Labour Party,
recognizing the extreme importance of Ireland
having an opportunity of delivering an unequivocal verdict in the most important election that
had been held for a generation, finally agreed to
withdraw its candidates and to allow the electorate
to decide on the political question only. The
decision was conclusive on the question. Out of
106 members returned for Irish constituencies, 73
were Sinn Fein candidates, pledged to abstention
from the English Parliament and to the claim of
Irish independence.

## CONCLUSION.

The months before the European War broke out saw Nationalist Ireland practically unanimous in its support of the Home Rule legislation of the Liberal Government, ready to be reckoned as a part of the British Empire, prepared to acknowledge the supremacy of the Imperial Parliament, content with an Irish Parliament charged only with the control of a number of matters of domestic concern. Though the policy of the Home Rule Act had been definitely and deliberately adopted by the English electorate, it was defeated by threats of armed resistance on the part of a minority of Irishmen, backed by promises of support from a minority of Englishmen, and by the refusal of the Liberal Government either to vindicate its own constitutional authority or to appeal to the country to do so for it. The Government put itself in the position of seeming to prefer in England the conciliation of its enemies to the satisfaction of its friends, and in Ireland to acknowledge the claim of a minority to veto the legitimate expectations of the majority. Occupying this position at home, it plunged into a war in Europe to vindicate "international morality" and "the rights of small nations," as a protest against the doctrine that the force of arms is superior to the force of justice and law. The month after the war ended saw

Nationalist Ireland still claiming and still denied (in obedience to the same obstructing forces) the right of self-determination: but the self-determination sought was no longer that in which before the war it had been content to acquiesce. It held that the war, which it had done something to win, had secured to the weaker nationalities (if the public and reiterated professions of the victors were not meant deliberately to deceive the world as to their intentions) the right to their own national existence, independent of the claims and the interests of the stronger nations by whom they had been subjugated. It held that during the war the rights, the interests, the feelings and the liberty of Ireland had been treated by the English Government with so much indifference and disdain as to make the future subordination of Ireland to English domination a prospect distasteful to Irishmen and a position injurious to Irish interests. It revived the claim of Ireland to independence, declaring that it was justified alike by history and by the common consent of Europe and America, and as a first step in the assertion of that claim refused for the first time since the Act of Union to send representatives to sit in the English Parliament. The forces which produced so serious an alteration in the attitude of Ireland have been described in the foregoing pages.

At the end of the war the only part of Ireland whose political outlook remained unaltered was the Unionist North-east. Upon the indurated surface of its political conscience nothing that had happened either in Ireland or out of it had produced the least effect. Alone in Europe the Ulster Unionist seemed to regard the war as a detachable episode with (so far as he was concerned) no political implications. He adopted the same standpoint, used the same language and expected it to meet with the same approving response from the same people. The changed attitude of other people was attributed by him to treachery, to disloyalty, to lack of fixed principle. By an adroit use of his opportunities during the war he managed to secure his position: he could point to the loyalty alike of those of his political faith who had enlisted and of those who had not enlisted: the former had done their duty to the Empire—the latter had performed their duty to the Government by providing it with a perpetual incentive to the conscription of Ireland. He had collected "pledges" from all who cared to give them that his position would be respected. To rely upon the " pledge" of a politician as a bulwark against the advance of political ideas may seem a somewhat imbecile proceeding: but it was not in his case so imbecile as it looked. He was shrewd enough to see that what European statesmen were doing was not by any means in accordance with what they were saying, and he decided (distrusting " ideas" of all kinds) to stake his future upon the relative permanence of things as they were rather than upon the doubtful advent of things as they ought to be.

Sinn Fein was the opposite of all this. It appealed alike from force and from fact to an ideal justice. Unable to win independence from a power both strong enough to coerce it and

interested for economic and military reasons in
retaining its hold upon Ireland, it refused to ask
for " pledges" which it felt sure would be broken,
even if given, it refused to plead its case before a
court whose interests were engaged against it in
advance. It preferred to appeal to its rights,
though there was no tribunal before which its plea
could come. It hoped that at the Peace Conference
the principle of self-determination could not be
insisted upon as against Germany, without Germany claiming that it should be acknowledged in
the case of Ireland. To its dismay and (it would
seem) to its surprise Germany was not represented
at the discussions : the Peace was dictated by a body
in which none but the victors were represented
and of which the object was not so much to establish a principle as to enforce a settlement, even
at the risk of establishing a precedent. The claim
of Sinn Fein that Ireland should be represented at
the Conference as an interested party was brushed
aside, contemptuously by the representatives of
England and France, shamefacedly by the representative of America. The League of Nations
which the Peace Conference set up was expressly
constructed to prevent interference with the
sovereign rights of its chief members as they
existed at the time it was constructed: the right of
England to retain whatever dominion it pleases
over Ireland is guaranteed by the League of
Nations in advance. Disappointed of the hopes
placed in the Peace Conference and the League of
Nations, Sinn Fein has to rely either on the interference in its favour of some Power whose friend-

ship England cannot disregard (an interference rendered less easy than it was by the very League of Nations which was expected to make it easier) or on the gradual and silent force of European opinion, or on the result of some future war.

Sinn Fein takes its stand upon the proposition that Ireland is a nation and upon the assertion that all nations have a just claim to independence. The proposition cannot be controverted except by arguments which go to prove that no such thing as a nation exists, and the assertion that all nations have a just claim to independence is like the assertion that all men have a right to be free: each is admitted in principle, but the principle is subject in practice to so many modifications that to say that a nation is free is to say what may mean as many different things as there are nations called free. A nation may be politically free and economically dependent, or vice versa: each of these conditions may be of various degrees on each side: and each of these again may be combined with varying degrees of moral, social and intellectual dependence.

Sinn Fein aims at the complete political, the complete economical and the complete moral and intellectual independence of Ireland. It has first to secure independence of England, and, having secured that, to avoid falling into dependence on any other Power. Its immediate problem is the means of securing independence of England. To induce England to acknowledge the independence of Ireland (to force her being out of the question, unless allies are to appear in the future) is no solution, as is abundantly proved by the history of their relations: the independence acknowledged in 1783 was recalled in 1800 and has been denied ever since. To induce the League of Nations, as at present constituted, to acknowledge the independence of Ireland is out of the question: if it were reconstituted so as to make it possible for it to do so, mere recognition of independence would be useless, unless the League were in a position to guarantee that it would continue to be recognized.

The means at the disposal of Sinn Fein at present hardly seem adequate to accomplish its object. It may bring about the moral and intellectual independence of Ireland: it may secure a certain measure of economic independence: but to secure political independence, in face of the forces ranged against it, seems impossible. But what it cannot do for itself may in the future be done for it by the moral forces of which it is a manifestation. It may in the future be recognized by the conscience of mankind that no nation ought to exercise political domination over another nation. But that future may still be as remote as it seemed in the days of the Roman Empire.